THE TOWER SERIES OF ANGLO-IRISH STUDIES III

GENERAL EDITOR ROGER MC HUGH

JACK B. YEATS
A CENTENARY GATHERING

The portrait of Jack B. Yeats reproduced is by Brian O'Doherty.

Jack B. Yeats

A Centenary Gathering

by SAMUEL BECKETT, MARTHA CALDWELL,
BRIAN O'DOHERTY, ERNIE O'MALLEY,
SHOTARO OSHIMA, MARILYN GADDIS ROSE
& TERENCE DE VERE WHITE

Edited with an Introduction by
ROGER MC HUGH

THE TOWER SERIES
OF ANGLO-IRISH STUDIES III

THE DOLMEN PRESS

Set in Plantin type with Perpetua display, and printed and published in the Republic of Ireland at the Dolmen Press, 8 Herbert Place, Dublin 2

1971

Distributed outside Ireland, except in the U.S.A. and in Canada by Oxford University Press.

SBN 85105 205 3

copy 2

CONTENTS

JACK B. YEATS

1871-1957

by Roger McHugh

'There is too much old chat about the Beautiful', Jack Yeats once said. He believed that the Beautiful is the affection that one feels for a person or thing, in life or in art; that to love life is to capture some intense moment of the enjoyment of life and to pass it on to others who can share it if they wish. This may be romantic but it is also engagingly human, characteristic of an artist who believed that a painter's development begins with the word 'man' and ends with the words 'true painter'. The few generalisations he made about art are challenging and refreshing. 'No one creates', he wrote; 'the artist assembles memories'. I think that he meant that the intense moment is always past but can be recaptured by trained observation, memory and technique. This is the primary business of the artist, but painting is also 'the freest and greatest means of communication we have', unlike language which, he seems to have thought, (even while he was writing his discursive books) is on its last legs in this age beforested by mass media, today's truthful antennae producing tomorrow's bogs of misunderstanding. Segovia's prayer —'Lord, I am not worthy of thy glory; please leave me here'— might have been his prayer, for he loved life and thought that the finest paintings had 'some of the living ginger of life in them.'

His earliest experience of this living ginger of life was in Sligo for, although born in London, he spent his childhood from his eighth to his sixteenth year there in charge of his grandparents. The Pollexfens and the Middletons would have given him a certain affection for Sligo, as well as an enthusiasm for ships and even for pirates; but more important was his actual sharing as a boy in the life of the people. Nominally he attended school but his school-going was more

7

honoured in the breach than in the observance. He preferred to play around the quays and the streets, inspecting with due reverence sea captains, sailors and pilots, or at country fairs and sports observing and sketching small farmers, pig-jobbers, worried shopkeepers, untamed tinkers, shouting ballad-singers, exultant jockeys surrounded by triumphant or sullen wild faces, or the stirring arrivals of Bianconi long-cars, of bands, of circuses. He said later in life that the two most stirring sights were 'a man ploughing and a ship on the sea'. The normal contained its own kind of adventure. But to the observant boy adventure often took more spectacular shapes. A quarrel or a song could unleash extravagant gesture, dramatic confrontation, or a swaggering sea-captain or tinker could set a quiet street agog with the expectation of violence, a prelude perhaps to song or story around the hearth.

In his introduction to the 1945 Exhibition of Jack B. Yeats's paintings Ernie O'Malley gives a vivid impression of the Sligo people and their wild and changing setting. Young Yeats's memory was a storehouse of potential pictorial treasure by the time he rejoined his family in London in 1887.

From childhood he had been fond of drawing. As a boy he had chalked sketches on the walls and pavements of Sligo town. In London he attended various art schools, including that of South Kensington, and gained, it seems, a certain trueness of line from formal training. But even at sixteen he had already started his career as a professional illustrator. W. B. Yeats recorded in a letter of 11 April, 1888 that Jack's first printed drawing, 'a drawing of fairies' had appeared in the *Vegetarian* a few days before. This paper also published stories by W. B. Yeats and his sister Elizabeth, illustrated by Jack. Gradually the demand for his work increased. He illustrated school-books, newspapers, periodicals, comic-cuts, racing papers. At twenty he announced to his surprised father his engagement to a fellow art-student, Mary Cottenham White from Devon, and after three years' hard work he was able to marry. They settled in Surrey in 1894 and moved to Devon in 1897, where they remained until

1910. During that period of his life, Jack visited Italy and France briefly, America for almost two months, but his most frequent visits were to Ireland. Where England gave him many subjects for his illustrations and sketches, Ireland provided almost all those for the drawings and water-colours which he exhibited between 1871 and 1910 in Dublin and London.

The painters who exhibited at the Royal Hibernian Academy at that time were either English or Irish imitators of the Leightons and the Poynters, titled men who set the standard. 'It was into their varnished world where it was nice to see a bit of Normandy or something from Surrey painted by an Irish artist' wrote C. P. Curran, 'that Jack Yeats broke with his troop of tinkers and maggie-men, jockeys and drovers, pig-jobbers and purse-proud horse-dealers, stout farmers and seafaring men, the whole life of a little western town by the sea. It was very exciting but was it art? It did not look a bit like Poynter or Watts or Albert Moore. It was good fun like the playacting of the Fays and the Allgoods but was it art?' The viceregal set were sure that it was not. They had cold-shouldered John Butler Yeats because of such Fenian friends as John O'Leary: now they uneasily turned their backs on his son's depiction of the Irish scene, on the vital medley of humanity and horses at Ballinasloe Fair, on the quieter studies of Ballycastle Bay or Downpatrick Head, or the six ragged members of the Pound Street Band ascending a village hill as if they were storming a city.

Today, of course, we have the advantage of hindsight and, if we master the jargon, can talk of the draughtmanship of these works, of their bold clear lines and simple direct colouring, of the way in which landscape is used as an appropriate setting for the human figure. All this would be true enough but would miss their particular magic and I am reminded of Yeats's own remark that if one could ask some artist of the past, say Botticelli, why he had painted his Venus, he might reply in terms of the technical arrangement of colour, of light and shade, but he would not be telling

9

the real truth: the real truth would be that he had painted it 'because she was such a damn fine gal'. This might be hidden from the artist himself but the particular clairvoyance or vision that lifts an artist above his technique would unconsciously reveal it. Following his own lead about the affectionate zest for life that is the basis of artistic achievement, I think that people untutored in technique but with some sensitivity can catch the essential elements of those early works. Some of them depict individuals, a farmer, a ballad-singer, a ganger and so on — but in such a way as to capture some essential quality which lifts the picture above its particulars. A tinker is painted in black garb which is set against the black of rock and the dark sky, relieved by a glimpse of white sea-foam. His wild eyes gleam from a 'black-avised' narrow face; he seems the embodiment of some wild night-spirit. The line drawing of the 'Squireen', bowler-hatted, gloomily assertive, owes much to the sharp, sure vertical lines of his coat and umbrella set against the curve of road, wall and mountain. The solidity of two pig-buyers in their heavy clothes is emphasised by the flat sunlit flag-stones on which they stand; two solid men, one bluff, one crafty, ready for the day's business as they leave the little railway-station. The simple colour-prints often catch some instant of wonder; a boy reins in his red pony as he stops to look at a black ship on a calm blue sea, or another lad swings his horse round the red marking-flag on brown, flat sand, the curve of the horse echoed by the curve of the rivulets of the tide. The vitality of crowds at fair or market is conveyed as much by contrast of swirling and static lines as by dramatic contrast of expression or the setting of appropriate landscape. Straight landscape painting, though comparatively rare in these early works, also has a dramatic quality, perhaps in the thrust of dark rock into the gleaming surge of sea. Always there is the living zest of life conveyed, even though the scene be a quiet one of a melodeon player in a drifting boat or a small boy inspecting a circus poster.

In 1910 Jack Yeats and his wife settled in Ireland, living first in Greystones then in Donnybrook, finally in Fitzwilliam Square. While W. B. Yeats disliked 'the daily spite of this unmannerly town' Jack liked Dublin's intimate warmth. In Devon he and his wife had spent a dozen years without knowing their neighbours; Greystones was 'neither town, country nor suburb' but Dublin suited them. Apart from its streets and quays and its convenience for expeditions to the West, it had become a centre of political ferment, which interested the painter more than its literary ferment. His sense of national identity, perhaps stemming from his father, had quickened as he travelled the West with Synge in 1905, or seven years before, when he attended the 1798 centenary celebrations at Carricknagat. Now the Dublin strike of 1913 inspired some of his work, he attended the funeral of O'Donovan Rossa, Pearse provided the inspiration for 'The Public Orator'. He thought that the Sinn Fein Movement had some living ginger in it and went to Kerry to learn Irish. Ireland, he thought, was a nation ready to start, once given the chance. Then came the Great War, the Rising, the Troubles, the Civil War. Ernie O'Malley, Republican guerrilla fighter (and his close friend) thought that the painter's work was assisted by the tensions of that time. Certainly some of the best paintings of this middle period came out of it; 'Bachelor's Walk (1915) 'Communicating with Prisoners' (1924), 'The Funeral of Harry Boland' (1922). The west continued to supply him with subjects all through those years; winnowers and kelp-gatherers, ships and horses, an island funeral. He was now passing deliberately from illustrative and descriptive painting to pure oil painting, was discovering himself as a colourist, as if his preoccupation with Ireland was calling out his full originality. Landscape now gives an extra tone to the human subject; reciprocally, figure to landscape. Both begin to blend; 'Early Sunshine' (1924) with its wonderful yellows, blues and reds shows this kind of merging of the human observer with sky and sea. Yet it was painted in the same year as 'Communication with Prisoners', which is much more conventional in style.

Jack Yeats believed that it was the duty of the artist to avoid conventions, even when the conventions were his own invention. When a Japanese visitor in 1938 commented on his later style, he replied that any real artist must necessarily change and spoke of the contrast between James Joyce's style in the Anna Livia Plurabelle episode which forms part of *Finnegans Wake*. It was an apt comparison. Joyce himself made the same comparison between his work and Jack's and bought two of his pictures of the Liffey. He had seemed to have gone as far as he could with language in *Ulysses* but had gone on to exploit its associative dream-qualities, to combine its mythical, legendary, historical, symbolic and realistic overtones in a new evocative style, heralded by the musical Sirens episode and the weaving dream of Molly Bloom with which Ulysses had concluded seventeen years before *Finnegans Wake*.

Jack Yeats's work during his last thirty years of painting provides as exact a parallel to this process as one can expect in two different art-forms. During that period he fulfilled himself as a 'true painter' whose greatest talent was in colour. Colour now dominates his work, acquires a flowing vitality reflecting the emotional drive which is evident also in the vigorous strokes of brush or of palette-knife with which it is applied. This fluidity is sometimes used to help the effect of motion of horse and rider, of sea and sky, as in 'The Wild Ones' (1947) or 'Night Coming Out of the Sea' (1951); it also gives a curiously evocative quality to human shapes which merge with and suddenly seem to emerge from the landscape, as in 'Tinker's Encampment — the Blood of Abel', while in 'Death for Only One' (1937) land and sky surround the still figure on the ground with changing time and changing nature, in which the standing figure who does reverence is involved until his own time comes round. It would be difficult to say whether the two figures, the landscape or the colour contribute most to the splendid desola-

12

tion of this painting, so well is the harmony between all its elements preserved.

The artist assembles memories . . . but memory, although founded on the feelings of the heart and the observation of the eye is not a card-index file. Each individual memory in that storehouse has its own associations but tends to acquire the associations of like memories. An accumulation of them may cause the artist, through 'clairvoyance' or subconscious thought, or whatever term one cares to substitute for what we normally call vision, or insight, to fuse many associations into the context of one subject. So themes which Jack Yeats had treated naturalistically or with clear definition in his early years — horses, circus clowns, travelling players, coaches — acquire symbolic overtones in his late oil paintings. Horses or seas become freedom itself. In 'In Memory of Bianconi and Boucicault' (1938) a cluster of barn-stormers around a Bianconi long-car convey at once the adventure of travel and of melodrama, the nostalgia of bygone times, and the tattered grace, gaiety and loneliness of the outcasts, the unusual ones. Sometimes Yeats gives fancy its head. 'California' is not the California of his time, if he ever saw it. It is the California of the primal American vision of adventure, in which the sight of a pretty woman is adventure enough. 'Helen' (1937) is one painting for which he bothered to provide an explanation (for Shotaro Oshima, his Japanese visitor). It was a product of his fancy, he said, based on the legend of 'the face that launched a thousand ships':

> You see Helen dancing in a boat . . . her golden hair is flowing like a flame to suggest her burning passion. The graceful curve of her body shows that she is dancing. At her feet crouches a figure, half brute and half human, with fixed eyes. It is recording the names of all the ships that are going down to the bottom . . . I tried to express a truth that is deeper than mere fact . . . this monster is writing down the names of the ships in Greek . . . even in mere fantasy there are often things inseparable from truth or things more real than reality itself.[1]

1 *W. B. Yeats and Japan.*

13

Lacking such explanations, some of his former admirers thought that his late style was perhaps due to failing vision, a notion which should have vanished if they observed the magnificent trueness of line of his illustrations for Frank O'Connor's *Lament for Art O'Leary* (1940) done three years after 'Helen'. Now that these paintings are highly valued and closely studied some critics perhaps tend to read into them symbols which are not intended; to see perhaps, 'The Great Tent has Collapsed' (1947) as connected with the collapse of Europe. On the other hand all but the most perceptive critics miss the overtones conveyed by apparently simple events depicted in evocative oils. 'He exposes the infinite possibility present in the simple meeting of two people', wrote Brian O'Doherty after seeing an American exhibition of Yeats's painting in 1965; 'he plumbs the mystery and loneliness of departures'. This quality may be seen in 'Night Coming Out of the Sea' or 'The Parting of the Three Ways' or 'Death for Only One'. Jack Yeats was not, even in old age, obsessed by death. Though it figures in several of his painting, it is something accepted as a part of nature, perhaps emphasising the vitality of life as the dark emphasises light; and to think of his greatest oil painting is to remember colour exploding into magnificent light or blending subtly into dark.

Samuel Beckett's highest praise is for the quality of light his paintings bring 'to the issueless predicament of existence'. Issueless? I doubt if Yeats would have agreed with the adjective. To create light and colour might well have seemed to him quite enough of an issue to be going on with.

Aspects of his art have been identified with various painters; his drawings with Sickert and Cruikshank, his paintings with Watteau, Daumier, the Impressionists, the Expressionists; I could add to the list the name of Asgrimur Jonnson, whose horses and skies remind me of Yeats, though I do not know if the latter had ever heard of his Icelandic contemporary. In truth he seems to have 'known his own know' and to have gone his own way from start to finish. He admired Goya but does not seem to have been influenced

14

by him. Social significance has been seen through binoculars in his studies of tramps and workers, tinkers, clowns and country lads; in short, in his identification with that member of the canine tribe identifiable with the Ireland of the first half of his life, the underdog. The artist often has an affinity with, and an affection for, such types, but with Yeats these issue in triumphant depiction, not in messages. A justifiable pride in his achievement perhaps has led us Irish at times to praise his work for its Irish, rather than for its great artistic qualities; he was our first great painter and found his real subject in the current Irish scene and in its association, including those of its fragmented culture. He thought that 'the true painter must be part of the land and of the life he paints' and this he was. The emphasis is on true painting, based on observation and memory; but lucky is the land whose national life can inspire such an artist. Ireland gave him, to use Dryden's phrase, 'a centre where to fix the soul', and now his spirit, manifest in colour, is part of the national conscious but has travelled outside it.

III

Beside this achievement the facts of official recognition seem comparatively unimportant. Elected a member of the Royal Hibernian Academy in 1916, his fame outside Ireland really began to spread through his association with the Victor Waddington Galleries in 1940. In 1945 came the Jack B. Yeats National Loan Exhibition at the National College of Art in Dublin, a wonderful display of the range of the seventy-four year old painter. In the same year was published Thomas McGreevy's *Jack B. Yeats,* the first book on his art since Ernest Marriott's perceptive work of 1911. Honours now crowded in; honorary degrees from T.C.D. and the National University of Ireland, British Arts Council exhibitions at the Tate and other galleries, honorary membership of the Adriatica Cultural Academy of Milan, the award of the Legion of Honour, retrospective exhibitions of his work in the United States and Canada. Public glory was paralleled by private sorrow. His father had died long before in New York, where he had emigrated after his wife's death. Now in the decade from 1939 to 1949 came the death of William Butler Yeats, of his two sisters and of Jack's wife, 'Cottie', with whom he had lived happily for over fifty years. Yet he might have echoed his brother's lines written under the threat of 'decrepit age':

> Never had I more
> Excited, passionate, fantastical
> Imagination, nor an ear and eye
> That more expected the impossible —
> No, not in boyhood, when with rod and fly,
> Or the humbler worm, I climbed Ben Bulben's back . . .

Some of his greatest paintings were painted after his eightieth year and he abandoned painting only two years before his death in 1957.

This tremendous vitality of Jack Yeats overflowed at intervals into literary activity. In his thirties he wrote plays for a miniature theatre, swashbuckling romantic melodramas, like *James Flaunty or the Terror of the Western Seas* or *The Bosun and Bob-tailed Comet*, delightful for children. In his sixties he resumed playwriting and wrote more serious experimental plays for the Abbey and its little Peacock Theatre; *Apparitions, Harlequins Positions, La La Noo* and some other shorter pieces. They are strange symbolic plays in which comedy often contains a trap-door to disaster, action disappears into casual colourful talk, good deeds end in sudden death for their performers and evils are as suddenly cured by friendship. They cast some light on the dramatic sense in the paintings which Brian O'Doherty stresses. Possibly the best of them is *In Sand* (Peacock Theatre 1949); a dying man, Anthony Larcson, leaves a bequest to ensure that a little girl will write with a stick on the sands his transient epitaph 'Tony we have the good thought for you still'. The little girl grows up, and marries, travels, grows old on a tropical island and continues her commemorative practice. Years after, the brown-skinned boys and girls of the island, which is in process of being

16

modernised for tourists, still trace the same words by the waters' edge, though the reason for the ritual has been forgotten. Through the imagination of a man long since dead, a talisman endures in a far country.

Was Jack Yeats here saying something about his paintings? Perhaps. But he also wrote a short 'conversation piece' for the stage, *The Green Wave*, in which two elderly gentlemen discuss a painting. One of them is a down-to-earth, businesslike person, who wants to know what the wave *means*. ' "I think it means just to be a wave" says the second: if that wave could speak it might say "I'm an Irish wave and the Irish are generally supposed to answer questions by asking questions", and the wave might ask you what was the meaning of yourself'.

The prose works which he wrote between 1930 and 1947 are just as puzzling. *Sailing Sailing Swiftly* (1933) and *The Amaranthers* (1936) are novels with some semblance of plot: though the former centres around three generations of one family, the author is liable to spend two pages describing the clothes of minor characters and to kill off his principals in as many sentences. Yet do not life and death sometimes seem as meticulous, as casual and as disproportionate as this?

The Amaranthers are a secret society of convivial Peter Pans whose chief aim is to enjoy the colour of life, even when it applies to the mixing of highly-coloured but lethal drinks or to witnessing incredible plotless melodramas. Having fled from organised society to an Indian 'almost-island' they are rescued by an eccentric Irish millionaire with a burning passion for 'come-all-yous' and steam-powered locomotives. Jack Yeats's five other books follow the pattern of his first, *Sligo* (1930), which has no plot whatsoever but simply follows the stream of memory and its random associations. They are prose sketch-books of memory. He wrote *Sligo*, he said, 'to jettison memories'. But the driftwood is highly coloured; memories of London circuses and boxing-matches, of Irish horse-races and fairs, of the Liffey at low tide, of snatches and titles of ballads, of the 'gay folly' of bonfires, flow over each other, sometimes pausing for more

17

deliberate inspection; 'a pink-eyed albino with a rose red round in the middle of his white head reeling and weaving from the pavement to the roadway and back again and two sturdy citizens taking a sledge-hammer from the grip of a wild quayside man.'

Memory, they say, plays strange tricks; whenever it flags its capers are assisted by Yeats's prods of fantasy. A memory of hearing a blood-soaked account of a bull-fight being greeted by a refined lawyer's clerk with the response, 'Ah, it must be very nice', leads the author to imagine a very nice arras play, 'the people with the dagger behind the arras would of course be standing in front of the curtains up close to the footlights and every now and then driving their dagger through the curtain and inspecting the blade. Red for luck.' Reading *Sligo* or *Ah Well* or *And To You Also* is like listening to a rambling talker who doesn't give a rambling damn whether you listen or not but who produces at intervals some extravagant remark or vivid verbal sketch that makes you glad he has dropped in. His few literary commentators incline to mention Sterne, Joyce, Beckett and the playwrights of the Theatre of the Absurd. There seems to me to be some truth in this last reference, although I think he would have rejected strongly their underlying thesis of man's essential absurdity. Again, his discursive style, his stream of memory method and his occasional remarks in these books that words are on their last legs might seem to justify the other analogies, but I do not think that he took himself very seriously as a literary craftsman. In his last years he expressed the wish that his books would be forgotten and his paintings remembered. The former, I think, really were written to jettison memories, while the paintings organise and assemble them. So a more correct analogy is between his work as a painter and that of Joyce as a master of language.

IV

Perhaps the two polarities of Jack Yeats's personality are best expressed in his father's painting of him as a boy, in which the quizzical expression of his eyes express a sense of fun, and Laurence Campbell's head of him as an old man, which has a brooding, introspective, tragic quality. From W. B. Yeats's letters one gets the impression of Jack as a carefree youth, joking, shouting out nonsense rhymes which he had picked up in Sligo, but capable of facing long spells of hard work as an illustrator or of standing up to his father in excited argument. Where W. B. Yeats was a solitary bookish youth, uneasy in company, Jack seems always to have delighted in crowds. His father once rejoiced that 'Latin and Greek and learning never affected Jack, since by the mercy of God he never paid any attention to them'; he thought that Jack had escaped the critical atmosphere of London, in which W. B. grew up, by being brought up in Sligo. Later, public controversy was to change the elder brother, bringing a slightly combative look to his expression and forcing upon him the defensive armour of a dignity which he felt appropriate to a poet. In maturity Jack could write to his brother 'I know that I am the first living painter . . . I have the immodesty of the spearhead', but there was no public indication of this private certitude in the quiet, retiring, courteous man whom few Dubliners knew even by sight. Oddly enough it was the essentially shy W. B. who became the 'smiling public man' but, as his wife said, never really knew people, while Jack, who certainly knew people, acquired until his last years something of the anonymity of a crowd, and despite his tall, spare look of distinction, something of the unobtrusiveness of some of those signatures which lurk in odd corners of his early paintings.

I think that Terence de Vere White and Brian O'Doherty are correct in assuming that after W. B. Yeats became a Senator in the early days of the Irish Free State, there was perhaps a temporary alienation from Jack, who was sympathetic with Republican and socialist thought. He was never a political activist but his sympathies are implicit in the choice of some of his subjects; 'Communications with Prisoners', 'The Funeral of Harry Boland', 'Going to Wolfe Tone's Grave'; and his friendship with Ernie O'Malley was based

19

on the sharing of more than artistic values. I remember
going to him once to ask him to sign a petition for the
reprieve of some young Republicans condemned to be hanged
in the Six Counties and he signed it without hesitation.
About the same time he sent me a subscription to a fund to
pay the burial expenses of a wandering ballad-singer, a tall,
shock-headed, red-haired man who might have stepped out
of one of his paintings.

These are slight but perhaps revealing glimpses of his
personality. Intimate friends have recorded other aspects:
courteous, almost ritualistic hospitality, quizzical conversation, the occasional shaft of sardonic wit, as on that occasion
in 1935 when he recited a self-composed epitaph to the
United Arts Club, beginning:

> Under no stones
> Nor slates
> Lies Jack B
> Yeats . . . .

which I venture to think was a take-off of the lines written
by his famous brother 'To be carved on a stone at Thoor
Ballylee'.

I have seen one photograph of the two brothers together,
taken in the country when they were both advanced in years.
W. B. looks good-humoured but stands in a formal pose,
right hand on lapel, the left behind his back, looking a little
like a successful lawyer; the panama-hatted Jack leans
casually against a gate-post enjoying what may be a stick of
'candy-floss'—or perhaps a careless flower? For the rest
I can recall only a few glimpses of him in his old age,
wandering along the Dublin quays or along the canal
towards his 'winter quarters' in the Portobello Nursing
Home, where he died. In those days he wore a curiously-
shaped black hat with a large silver buckle, a long black
coat which accentuated his height. He looked like a
gaunt but kindly uncle out of some fairy-tale. As a person
he lives for me less in these glimpses than in his painting
'The Quiet Man' where a tall, sombrely-clad man stands

20

contemplating a glass of whiskey in a dark seaside pub. Outside are the gay colours of the sea, ships and flags. At any moment now he will down the yellow drop and get back to them . . . but now he is quiet. Ah well, we have the good thought for him still.

EDITOR'S NOTE

The studies by Brian O'Doherty, Marilyn Rose and Terence de Vere White were written and the chronology and bibliography by Martha Caldwell were contributed specially for this book. Samuel Beckett's two pieces appeared originally in *The Irish Times* (4 August, 1945) and in *Lettres Nouvelles* (April 1954). Ernie O'Malley's introduction was printed in 1945, while Professor Oshima's account of his interview was published in his book *W. B. Yeats and Japan* (Hokuseido Press, 1965). To all these writers or to their representatives I am deeply grateful, as to Anne and Michael Yeats and to the Cuala Press Limited for permission to use the illustrations.

THE PERSONALITY OF
JACK B. YEATS

by Terence de Vere White

Jack Yeats first entered my life in the late spring or early summer of 1917. My parents were then living at number 61 Marlborough Road, Donnybrook, a modest Victorian terrace house on a rather dreary road. It has changed very little in half a century. That first childish impression is now hopelessly vague. I can only recall a presence, unobstrusive, inspecting — we were moving out, the Yeatses were coming in — and whether he came into a nursery or schoolroom, or whether I got but a fleeting glimpse in the hallway, I cannot say. I can only recall a shadowy adult presence. But I vividly remember my mother's complaining. She was a house-proud woman; and she was complacent about her own taste. Mrs. Yeats had disclosed her intention of removing the Morris wall-paper of which my mother was fond (not original Morris papers, the imitation ones) and painting the walls instead. In 'hideous colours', my mother said afterwards; so she may have gone there to tea after the new tenants moved in.

I regret that in this first encounter there is no recollection of either awe or appreciation. There was, I fear, a depressing bourgeois smugness in Dublin at that time, a philistine attitude to artists in general (unless they showed at the Royal Academy and were mentioned in the Honours List). The word Bohemian was then much in use and was mildly pejorative. My mother had no doubt in her mind that her Morris paper was more attractive and more suitable for a house than Mr. Yeats's 'colours'. In fairness, let me say, that my mother's rooms exuded more comfort and cheer than the Yeats's flat, as I remember it, where the general impression was austere even when he became comfortably off.

My next recollection is a book of Irish fairy stories with

Jack Yeats's illustrations. Then ten years later I am at the Royal Hibernian Academy with my mother and a friend. They speak irreverently of the large Yeats pictures on view. He had recently adopted his expressionist technique and had departed from his illustrative method, at much the same time as his poet brother bade farewell to the fairy lyricism upon which his general popularity rested. Most people by then knew a drawing of a donkey by Jack Yeats. It was printed by the Cuala Press, which his sisters managed. The people who were disapproving of Bohemians would have wished that one Yeats should continue to reproduce that pretty little donkey, and the other the lake-isle of Innisfree, over and over again.

About the time I heard disrespectful comment about Yeats's latest pictures, I had entered Trinity College and had joined the College Historical Society. Jack Yeats used sometimes to come and take the chair at its meetings and even stayed to supper on ceremonial occasions. He was a familiar figure to older members, and I recall a cry — 'Tell us about Mark Twain!' — when he got up to speak. I cannot remember anything he said on the two or three occasions he presided; nor even the Mark Twain anecdotes. But I thought at the time that there was something very appropriate to his personality in the idea of Twain; and I still think that if Yeats had a predominating facet it was as a character in the world of Huckleberry Finn. He was rather sailor-like, but like a sailor in a boy's story.

He looked tall, but that was due to leanness rather than excess of inches. W. B. Yeats was a much larger man; and Jack never became portly, as the poet did. He was as thin as a rake. He had very little hair in my time — mere wisps — a long face and jaw and a curved forehead. 'Dome' is the usual simile for such frontispieces, but the word is not apt in Yeats's case. His skin was like old silk, stretched, but not creased, tussaud colour. Sometimes his cheeks grew dark red; but not when he was well and warm. (He was critical of red-faced men; and said of one of our common acquaintances with a perpetually high colour that he must be an ill-tempered man, and of another that he believed him to be a secret drinker. It was true, as it happened.)

In height he was, I suppose, something under six feet. He moved as if he was on deck and the sea was choppy. When he talked to one he put his head on one side and looked up as a bird does. (You can see the expression in a picture of him as a boy by his father in the National Gallery in Merrion Square). His eyes were blue and amber, and their expression was shrewd, kind and humorous. I place their characteristics in the proper order. The chin was long and the mouth had a sardonic twist, a family expression. It can be seen in the pencil-drawing J. B. Yeats did of W. B. as a child, and in his portrait of Lily Yeats. When he talked his mouth, which was wide but thin-lipped, lay open, as does a dog's, barking at another dog in the distance, ready to answer back if its bark is returned. There was a bleating, not a barking, quality in Yeats's quiet voice. It became more marked when he fell into a mood of fantasy, when his meaning became increasingly difficult to catch. His family, he told me, must have come originally from Yorkshire; and Yeats was, he thought, a variation of 'goat'. Like many of his theories I doubt if this one had any factual basis; but it is interesting because, if one is trying to picture what Yeats was like, one should imagine a gentle, lean, and very courteous goat without that goat-look in the eye which is the repellent feature of goats. When Yeats was talking, slowly, with his mouth wide-open, he made the gentle bleating sound I have described. It was soporific; and I have sometimes, when alone with him on a winter evening, undergone a Lewis Carroll sensation of metamorphosis, like that of the Queen into a woolly sheep.

I knew Yeats best when he was a very old man, and woolliness was not at all the impression on a first meeting. I recall the attentiveness of the eye, the total absence of condescension, the grace of manner. In those days people were more inclined to stand upon their advantages in casual contacts; age dominated youth; difference of social position was at once apparent. Yeats was entirely free of every pre-

24

tension of that character. His presence was ageless and classless, not as if he was unaware of such differences, but as if he was above them. He was the least vulgar of men. I doubt if anyone was ever rude or impertinent to him.

He always dressed in the same manner, in dark clothes with a black cravat. A long neck showed over the collar. His overcoat came to his heels and had large sleeves, the kind you see in pictures of coachmen long ago, and he had a large black felt hat. In the sleeve of his coat a notebook fastened to his wrist by elastic was secreted. This enabled him to make drawings in the shelter of his capacious sleeve. He looked, in fact, very like a figure in his early drawings of country characters.

Jack Yeats was the youngest of the children of John Butler Yeats and Susan Pollexfen. He kept his age a secret. He told me once that somebody had asked him what it was and he had refused to say. 'I was not an infant prodigy and I'm not going to be a senile prodigy.' But he was reticent, not to say secretive about most things. He was a man to whom one hesitated to put any question concerning himself or his work, nor do I recall him ever asking me a personal question, although we spoke intimately, particularly at the time when Mrs. Yeats died. I saw a great deal of him then; but the form his confidence took was to say exactly what he thought about our various acquaintances. He did not talk about himself or expect you to talk about yourself. He was proud. I was told that he disliked any discussion of his painting. This led to not a little insincerity at gatherings in his room. Everyone praised everything equally.

An artificial rose was fastened to the top of his easel. This is shown in the painting of his studio, formerly owned by Richard McGonigal. The picture was bought after his death by Victor Waddington, and was one of a series of rose paintings. For both Yeats brothers the rose had a symbolical significance. But there was a distinction between their employment of it, which was one of the marks of the essential difference in their natures. The poet used it romantically in his lyrical phase, and later linked it to his rambles through occult, eastern and Grecian philosophies and other esoteric playgrounds. For Jack Yeats, if 'a rose is a rose is a rose' was not quite the whole story, his attitude to the flower was less egocentric, his devotion more consistent than his brother's. He was content to look at the rose; to love it for its own sweet sake.

In his book *Sligo* there is a long list of the names of ballads; and anyone who is at all acquainted with Yeats's art will recognise the titles he liked to put on his paintings among them. One is 'This Conversation took place under the Rose'. Yeats painted a very attractive, romantic, Fragonardish picture of a circus scene with that title when he was past seventy. A characteristic explanation of the rose on his easel would have been that all his paintings were, in a manner, conversations 'under the rose'. It would not have been in character for him to have been more esoteric than that.

We know that Yeats, though born in London when his father was living near Regent's Park, was sent to his Pollexfen grandparents in Sligo and grew up there. He got, I should think, a sparse formal education. His conversation had no tang at all of academic adornments. His education was largely conducted by his own eyes and directed however unconsciously, towards the creation of an artistic personality.

A small child with old people, he was thrown very much upon himself. He was always, we are told, cheerful and self-reliant, the sort of boy who gets on very well with the busy because he is companionable, observant and does not get in the way. Sligo had a character of its own. It was a town with a merchant population that was largely protestant. W. B. Yeats was inclined to magnify and romanticise his Pollexfen relations as Wilde his eccentric parents. All came of solid rather than glamorous stock. In Ireland there was always a sharp difference between town people and county people. They did not mix socially; and the amount of conventional amusement available for Yeats in Sligo was, I can guess, meagre. He had to find his own entertainment; and he found it on the docks and the strands, looking at gypsies and fairs and circuses and flapper races; and in the long evenings in books, books about pirates and adventures.

When he was sixteen he returned to London and studied in various art schools and supported himself — the family was very poor always — by making drawings for the comic papers. In London he sought out much the same world as he had left behind him in Sligo. Never was a man so much of a piece. He haunted the docks, boxing matches, trotting races, music halls. It was an extension of the life he had built up for himself; to what extent it was the result of circumstances, of being thrown upon his resources, of having no money to spend, and how much was an inborn inclination, who can say?

Once in conversation I heard him say that the modern child loses a lot from the dethronement of the father as family oracle. He had learned much from his own father's incessant table talk; but, then, very few people have had such a remarkable father or one who was such a remarkable talker. Nevertheless, Jack Yeats was probably much less influenced by his father than the poet was. For one thing he was not with him so much, and there is no evidence of a correspondence such as that which the old Yeats kept up with his sometimes unresponsive elder son. Because W.B. had taken words as his medium of expression the father may have been more concerned to influence his thought. Then it is probable that Jack was not of a didactic turn. He was up and doing rather than talking; he listened, no doubt, but made no attempt to discuss. He had his own ideas about everything; but he did not invite argument, and it was not very easy to argue with him because his ideas were so often whimsical. His nature was more affectionate than W.B.'s and, if entirely self-sufficient, he was not so self-centred. The poet, walking about, or even in company when he wasn't holding forth, would be seen to move his lips in silent recitation; Jack Yeats was ever on the alert; he missed nothing. In a gathering where someone was left out of the conversation if Jack Yeats was present, I can imagine him singling out the neglected person for attention. Not so W.B.

27

In the poet's autobiographies, Jack is rarely mentioned. I do not think he moved at all in the circles in London that his brother has written so much about. York Powell, the Oxford professor, a close friend of their father, is one of the few persons mentioned in the poet's autobiographies of whom I ever heard Jack Yeats speak. Neither did he get caught up in politics as his brother did through the old Fenian John O'Leary who introduced him to Maud Gonne.

Jack married very early, while still an art student, and his early years were spent in England. That period in Devon when the young couple lived in a cottage near to the Masefields has been recorded in many water-colour paintings. They were frugal, happy, innocent years. Jack Yeats's marriage to Mary Cottenham White was in complete contrast to his brother's manner of life, his hopeless poetic passion for Maud Gonne, his love affairs and his marriage late in middle-age. Jack and his wife had no children: this left no cloud, if it was regretted. As is sometimes the case in childless marriages it may have drawn the couple even closer to one another. Jack Yeats's boyishness, his Huckleberry Finn side, his pirate games and cow-boy obsessions, were given rein, not abandoned after marriage. Mrs. Yeats adored him and seemed intent to preserve him as he was. Whether it would have been possible to affect any alteration in so clearly defined a personality is a question; but she was not a wife who wanted to influence her husband. They were like a brother and sister keeping alive the spirit of nursery days.

Old Mr. Yeats once said that Jack was really the poet of the family. But he does not seem to have influenced Jack greatly. A letter is extant in which he deplores his son's neglect of instruction in drawing and prophesies that he will regret it; but his wife is so adoring that it is impossible to drive this uncomfortable truth home.

Young Mrs. Yeats had some private means; and in the early years of the century a couple in a country cottage with no children, no vices, and simple tastes could live on very little. John Masefield, sailor-poet, was one of the people with whom Jack Yeats lived in comradeship; but he never spoke of him with any great affection, and I doubt that they kept up their friendship. Mrs. Masefield was possibly the fly in the ointment. Yeats spoke of her as if she had been.

In any event it is a mistake to take too absolute a line about friendship. It is generally assumed that the young fall in and out of love and this is no reflection on the characters of those concerned; but a falling off in friendship is generally regarded as a sign of coldness of heart or fault of character. People are not apt to confess that they have tired of friends; it sounds like a reflection on themselves. As a result many friendships are kept going like a fire in wet weather by bellows action instead of being allowed to sizzle out without fuss. The young Masefield and the young Yeats enjoyed sailing paper-boats, exchanging yarns, making up private games and toy theatres. As septuagenarians they would have found that these diversions palled when all they had in common was a memory of dead summers.

Toy theatres were much more in fashion in those days than now when puberty coincides with cocktails. The difference between Yeats and other men was his fidelity to childish games—perhaps I am doing an injustice to the many men who keep up through life a craze for trains. The theatre was a lifelong addiction. I have said he frequented music-halls; but his interest in them was idiosyncratic. I don't think he greatly cared about the quality of the performance. I own a sketch book which he gave me with 'London June 1907' on the fly-leaf. It contains drawings of George Robey, 'the white-eyed Kaffir', and other music-hall celebrities of the day. He enjoyed their songs and didn't mind if they were silly, as he enjoyed the ballads of Sligo. His toy theatres were another matter. He painted the scenery, and he took it all seriously — as a child plays a game seriously. Many of his paintings are stage sets, even when he took to oils, halfway through his life.

The evidence upon which I rely for this phase in Yeats's life is a little paper-covered book he gave me, 'Jack B. Yeats His Pictorial and Dramatic Art by Ernest Marriott, containing a chart of Pirate Island by Jack B. Yeats and a portrait'.

It was published by Elkin Mathews in Vigo Street in 1911, being the text of a lecture given to the Manchester Literary Club. It is a source from which as much as Yeats ever disclosed about his life can be drawn. It tells us that he studied at several art schools; South Kensington, Chiswick, the West London, and at Westminster under Professor Fred Brown. Technique merely as technique does not exist for him'. In that sentence we may see the germ of his father's complaint. Did he get bored at the schools?

'When he was seventeen years of age,' Mr. Marriott continues, 'he drew for some of the halfpenny comic papers, and attended running-matches nearly every Saturday, making drawings for a sporting paper, *Paddock Life*. Later on he worked for *Chums, Fun* and other papers. These drawing were faggots to boil the pot. Seldom was he free to illustrate the things he himself thought funny. I know one person, however, who thought this early work the fountain-head and last expression of his humour. No regrets could be keener than mine that I have not preserved those halfpenny journals which in early youth I purchased solely for the delight of beholding in all their reckless glory the fanciful figures of Jack Yeats. I did not at the time understand why his work was more attractive than that of the other contributors. It was the difference between mediocrity and a great talent allied to a Celtic temperament that gave his work the flavour and savour which were so alluring'.

Mr. Marriott lists the titles of Yeats's books and plays for the miniature theatre to date:

1. 'The Bosun and the Bob-tailed Comet'.
2. 'A Little Fleet'.
3. 'The Treasure of the Garden'.
4. 'The Scourge of the Guelph'.
5. 'James Flaunty, or the Terror of the Western Seas'.

'A Little Fleet' is a description of the various toy-boats made by young Jack Yeats and his chums. He gives an extract which I copy not so much as evidence of what Jack Yeats wrote at this time — a task outside my province — but for the glimpse it affords of his mind:

30

'The *Monte* was the first of our vessels and was made out of a flat piece of wood about five inches long. She had two masts and was rigged up as a fore and aft schooner . . . . She started from No Name Straits with wind and tide . . . . and bore away for mid-stream to avoid the *nifty* snags that lie at the foot of the bluff called Pirate's Leap, called that because a poet who had been a pirate was thinking about a poem when he ought to have been shoving the vessel off the rocks and so he fell in'.

Masefield wrote accompanying verses.

It all seems much closer to Peter Pan than to the tragic passionate atmosphere from which W. B. Yeats was drawing the inspiration for his verse. Jack was fiddling, it seems, while Willie was burning; fiddling during the last period in history when such a pleasant way to pass the time was possible. The horror of war and the pressure of prices keep even the romantic with his nose to the grindstone.

Yeats always had to work for a living. At first he got it by comic-cuts cartoons, later as an illustrator, and for many years a little drawing used to appear regularly on the last page of *Punch* signed 'W. Bird'. It was recognised as Yeats's work, but I never heard him mention it. There was nothing to be ashamed of in having contributed regularly to *Punch*; one can only surmise that Yeats resented it as a chore.

The Peter Pannery — how he would have resented that! — which entertained his early marriage years was much closer to his artistic life than the illustrations for which he was paid. He made up these toy theatres with cut-out casts and sold them at three guineas each. I have book-markers he gave me which have pirate scenes on one side and characters from Dickens on the other. Dickens was the writer I would expect Yeats to have enjoyed most. One side of him must have revelled in Micawber, another in Peggoty; and I don't think Yeats would have repudiated even Little Nell. But I never heard him once refer to Dickens; and I must assume that he fell out completely with England after 1916 and repudiated her with all her works and pomps. I recall the contemptuous tone in which he referred to Joseph

Conrad's account of how he went out in a boat to touch the side of an English man-of-war and of how he felt the better for the experience.

Conrad was a man of ships with a reverence for the British navy; but Yeats reserved his affection for pirate vessels. He would, I think, have spoken slightingly of Nelson. To what extent he disliked things British because they were the instrument of imperialism, law and order, and other grim things which his romantic boy-nature repudiated, whether he would have softened towards a Britain that was down and out, I cannot tell. I think everything to do with England became abhorrent to him. in a way that they never became for his brother who yet expressed his nationalist views openly. And I believe that the abhorrence was the reaction of a boy who has seen an act of violence in his youth. O'Connell, we are told, hated revolution all his life because he had seen Louis XVI and Marie Antoinette perish under the guillotine as a youth in Paris. Yeats, I believe, lived apart from the grim facts of life and had no taste for politics, but he came back to Ireland to live in Greystones, Co. Wicklow; and he was living in Ireland during the whole period when the issue of Irish freedom was being fought out.

There is a beautiful picture of his depicting a girl in a shawl dropping a flower into the basement of a house. This represents a girl paying tribute to her lover killed by the Scottish Borderers, who fired into the crowd on Bachelor's Walk in 1914. It was on the Sunday before the outbreak of the 1914-18 War. The *Asgard*, a yacht belonging to Erskine Childers, delivered a cargo of arms to the Volunteers at Howth in the morning. British troops were called out, but there was no fighting. However, on the way back to barracks the crowd taunted the soldiers and, it was alleged, threw stones at them. A young officer gave the order to fire, and a few people, including some women, were killed.

That incident alone — nobody was punished — was quite sufficient to make Yeats hate whatever gave those soldiers the power to commit such a wanton act. Because it was done

32

by Government servants he would have found it more hateful than any act of piracy. He was not, I think, really very fond of people in general. His whole heart belonged to his wife, and he had a strong sense of family loyalty. From the rest of the world he stood back, and even his friends, I believe, were not free from a certain scepticism of scrutiny; but he loved goodness. He loved the idea of children. He tried to retain the spirit of childhood and in this his wife helped. He could manufacture almost any theory to suit his fancies, but his eyes saw facts. And the facts that were laid out before them after his return to Ireland were that 1914 shooting on the Quays, the Rising of 1916, the Black and Tan years, and the Civil War. His paintings in relation to the period are chiefly of funerals; I distinctly remember one of wives looking up towards the tower of Kilmainham where their menfolk are imprisoned. He painted, to my knowledge, nothing to celebrate any of the fighting.

Having become emotionally involved, he was consistent when the treaty between the Irish representatives and the Coalition under Lloyd George signed in December 1921 was repudiated by Mr. de Valera, an act which led inevitably to Civil War. Jack Yeats took the side of the anti-treaty forces. He was not concerned with practical politics or economics. He lived simply. He never sold his soul. He had no use for compromise. Although he was much addicted to ceremony in matters pertaining to old customs — passing the port, say — he disliked the flummery of public office. Instinctively he rebelled against the pomp of power. In any event it was sufficient that the 'Irregulars' were further from the British than the 'Free Staters' for him to side with the uncompromising side.

The Civil War led to executions; and there was a definite breach between the Yeats brothers when W. B. fraternised with the Free State Government and entered the first Senate. W. B. Yeats in his poetry bewailed the effect of political abstractions on Maud Gonne and Constance Markievicz. Jack Yeats had no taste for abstractions either; both lamented the effect they had on personality. They drew the milk of

33

human kindness out of women's breasts and substituted vinegar.

I knew only the poet Yeats by hearsay; I knew Jack Yeats as well as a man much younger can know an older man whom he knows only when he is old. That it to say, I never saw Jack Yeats active, except in the matter of kindness. I give here two instances of that. We were talking about an old woman who had fallen on hard times. She had taught me as a child; Yeats remembered her in the theatre, where she had been at one time an energetic amateur of more pretension than distinction. I told him, without the least idea of involving him, that her former pupils had made a collection among themselves on her behalf. On the following morning I received a letter from Yeats enclosing £50 towards the fund. That was worth several times as much as it is as I am writing these words. On another occasion he asked me to call and gave me £25. A young artist whom he had heard of as being very ill was holding an exhibition. I was to go and buy pictures up to that amount and pretend they were bought by me. He never wanted to see them.

Servants liked him. The caretaker of the house in which he lived and his wife spoke of him with genuine affection and respect. Once when I was writing a piece about Thor Ballylee, near Gort, where W. B. Yeats lived in his tower, I chanced to meet an old man who remembered both the Yeats brothers and was accustomed to drive the poet to Lady Gregory's house at Coole, a few miles away. He said that W. B. never spoke a word during the drives or showed any awareness of his existence, but 'Mr Jack' was very friendly and nice to everyone. They liked to see him arrive to stay at the Tower.

W. B. Yeats liked pomp. The business of the Tower was itself, when coolly considered, highly pompous. He could 'get away with it'; and it fitted both his appearance and his philosophy, his essentially hierarchic view of life. It was one of his masks. Jack Yeats wore no mask. W. B. was always the eldest son, Jack the youngest of the family, an object of general affection upon whom no responsibility rests.

W. B. comported himself as one upon whom a great inheritance had descended or was about to descend. No son of a great house could have more consciously fitted himself for his ancestral role; and if (as George Moore relates) he said that by rights he would be Duke of Ormonde, he must have believed it in his heart's core. Even W. B.'s relation with the fairy kingdom had about it something of the diplomatic recognition one sovereign gives to another's domain. He apparently lacked the common touch. At what point did the brothers meet?

Both were well aware that they belonged to the gentry but Jack Yeats had no illusions about class; his pride, which was great, never took his brother's theatrical turn. Once, greatly daring, I asked him about this, and he replied quite simply that he believed W. B. to have been much concerned about the status of poets, and that his bearing was a demonstration on behalf of the dignity of the poets' calling. His own rôle was essentially different, he was an observer of life. He had to mingle with the crowd. He was fascinated by character.

Both men were ironical and, in their different ways, formidable. although Jack was so much more approachable. He was reserved rather than shy: W. B. Yeats was shy. He moved like a shy man. He was also self-conscious. Jack Yeats was not.

For all W. B. Yeats's fine words about aristocracy, both he and his brother exhibited much more of the characteristics one would naturally associate with merchants of good standing engaged in respectable trades. They were careful, exact and just in financial and business matters; through both their natures ran a strong streak of caution. W. B. Yeats's most celebrated explosions of public wrath were masterpieces of calculated timing, anger in a play. There was very little that was impulsive about either of them. W. B. might flirt with revolution but never carried a gun; Jack dreamed of pirates but never ran away to sea. After Maud Gonne had

35

let her house to W. B. Yeats when he arrived in Dublin with his bride, she came one day and asked to be allowed to stay. Yeats refused to take her in on the ground that his wife was soon expecting a child and he did not want to subject her to the strain of possible raids by the police or military.

P. S. O'Hegarty, whose grand-daughter married the poet's son, Michael Yeats, told me that on one occasion during the Black and Tan period he crossed the road to where Jack Yeats was living (in our former residence, 61 Marlborough Road) and asked him to take in young Sean MacBride who was 'on the run'. The police, O'Hegarty said, would probably search his house but they would not think of looking in Yeats's. Yeats refused. Possibly he was unimpressed by O'Hegarty's argument and saw it as a buck-passing operation. Nor did Sean MacBride have any claim on him. By that time Maud Gonne was estranged from his brother.

Many years later I happened to call on Jack Yeats and found him for once showing agitation. He told me that it was brought on by the thought of the morrow when he had to be present to see his nephew marry a grand-daughter of P. S. O'Hegarty. O'Hegarty was a very outspoken critic of the de Valera side at the time of the Civil War. The I.R.B. supported the Treaty; they followed Collins. Jack Yeats took the other side. But his partisanship was not, as I have said, so much political as emotional. He was talking to me once of Erskine Childers who was shot by the pro-treaty side. Childers was said by some to have been greatly under the influence of his American wife. After the execution Yeats called to condole with her. According to his own account he was led into a room in which the curtains were drawn and the widow was lying on a sofa. He began to say whatever he had come to say in the dreadful circumstances when a child came into the room, saluted and said 'The Republic lives on'. This was the eldest boy, now a Minister in the Irish Government. Yeats said he felt so sickened by the demonstration of false values — a child, his father a few hours dead, being taught to mouth abstractions — that he

36

found he had to go away, and he never felt able to call on Mrs. Childers again.

He was above all a tender-hearted man; his pictures are full of children and animals. They are never sad. Marriott noticed this in 1911: 'His sympathy with brute creation makes him refrain from representations of ill-treated or miserable animals, but if he finds it necessary for his purpose to draw a scraggy horse he comforts himself by giving it a wicked eye.'

I can date the real beginning of our friendship. In 1941 Jack had an exhibition of paintings in Contemporary Pictures, a gallery no longer extant in Upper Baggot Street. I happened to have in my pocket a cheque for £100, the largest amount I had ever owned at once, a fee from an intending apprentice. I found myself in front of a picture which excited me more than any picture I had ever seen by a living artist. The catalogue described it as 'Man in a Train Thinking', and the price was marked £100. The coincidence was too much, and I remember asking the lady in charge of the gallery if I could buy it. There is always an air of unreality about one's appearance in a new rôle. I had never spent more than a very few pounds on a picture. I was never to recapture the first fine careless rapture of that occasion. A few days later Yeats met me in the street. We had our usual few words; but this time he told me he was at home in his studio every Thursday, if I would like to come.

From that time on I became a fairly regular Thursday visitor. At first there used not to be more than a few; but as time went on the numbers grew. Yeats was only then coming into his own. The tide turned emphatically in his fortunes when Kenneth Clark, Director of the National Gallery, invited him to exhibit work in a two-man show with William Nicholson. It was an extraordinary combination; one so bold, the other so meticulous; an antithesis of manner and method. At the same time Clark wrote an article about Yeats for *Horizon,* a wartime literary magazine that enjoyed considerable prestige under the editorship of Cyril Connolly. Yeats concealed pleasure of achievement. He

37

believed in himself and accepted recognition as his belated due. He made no demonstration of pleasure about this exhibition, but I remember his unconcealed dissatisfaction with Clark's article. 'Always a pull-back,' he said, meaning that he never got unstinted admiration.

Here is what put Yeats out:

A comparison with the great poet, his brother, is irresistable. Both loved proud and passionate men who yield to the passion of an impulse; and they found such men in Ireland, where a crazy feudalism had left them nothing to lose, where tinned foods, building societies, the instalment system and the other modern means of destroying independence had hardly penetrated. The poet Yeats said that he wished to write ballads which should be on the lips of men who could not read, and praised 'So we'll go no more a roving' because it was great verse with the lilt of popular verse. But he could only find his way to a direct vernacular utterance by passing through labryrinths of myth and learning. Jack Yeats was there in a leap, and may seem to have reversed his brother's development, for his early work is in the style of popular ballads, and often actually illustrates them, whereas his later work is symbolic in its use of evocative colour, and makes no concession to the dull average eye. But the poet's long discipline, his painful search for a myth comprehensive enough to allow him to write simply, gave his work a certainty which his brother's painting lacks. Occasionally, even in the latest pictures, one catches sight of those naïve uncertainties of drawing which so much shocked me in the work of W. Bird. They are exhibited with engaging candour . . . .

One can see why Yeats was not enamoured of Clark's written verdict.

Earlier in that article the writer referred to the W. Bird drawings. 'They had more of the tricks of the trade, and in consequence looked to me very bad' and towards the close he referred to 'men of twice his natural talent' who had succumbed to the temptation to can art for export. In sum, he praised the artistic integrity of Yeats, jealously preserved 'on the other rim of European painting' and implied that the value of his work was more than the paintings of more gifted men (Orpen springs to mind) who had truckled to the taste of the market place.

Whether or not he felt the uncertainty about his work that Clark referred to in his *Horizon* article is an intriguing question. Certainly he did not discuss it and, as I have said, in his studio the practice was to praise everything. I never heard a note of criticism or comparison uttered by anyone in his presence. Nobody ever said 'I prefer this to that.' It was put about that Yeats was ultra-sensitive. I can only speak from my own experience. I once bought a picture of his which I afterwards — wrongly I think now — lost faith in. I mentioned this to Mr. Waddington who told me that Yeats would be hurt if he thought one had attempted to sell one of his pictures. During a period when I was seeing a great deal of Yeats, just about the time of his wife's death in 1947, I must have confessed my lapse. He gave no sign of distress, but told me to bring the picture back and choose another. He spoke of his methods in a practical sort of way. Most painters, he said, begin with the foreground and work back; he operated on the opposite principle. Many painters, I believe, keep the whole picture in progress for the sake of unity. I asked him once about his materials and he simply said that he bought the best. He never, I should think, experimented in mixing his own colours. In fact there is cracking in some of the reds in his paintings, as there is in some Osbornes. I never saw any cracks in a Nat Hone painting, but then he never made impasto effects.

As to fault-finding: one evening he took out a bundle of watercolours and showed them to me. I asked if I might buy one of a Devon horse fair. There is a wet patch in the trees where, perhaps, the brush was too much loaded. He looked at that and asked me if I would like him to do something about it. I said not, I would take it as it was. Another time I was alone with him in his studio when he had on the easel a picture which was used to illustrate Clark's *Horizon* article 'Had I the Wings of a Swallow' it is called. A girl is standing up in a half-empty railway carriage. There is something unsatisfactory about her nose, even allowing for

Yeats's summary way of depicting figures. I don't know how I got round to saying so; but I did. At this moment, according to the briefing I had had, from Thomas McGreevy in particular, the earth should have opened. But it remained closed and Yeats, as I remember it, merely studied the picture and said he would consider the nose. The next time I saw him he said he had been working on it but had come to the conclusion that there was nothing more he could do about it. Again, he was not in the least offended, and he sounded completely human and natural.

He was courteous about visiting exhibitions of other painters; and I remember him saying to me once that it was much easier to find faults than to discover merits, and that his plan at any exhibition was to look for these. But he refused to show with other Irish contemporaries. He was left out of at least one exhibition because he insisted that he must be shown alone or not at all. He told me to keep out of groups and not to accept positions on committees for good causes. 'They only want to use you', he said. If ever there was an individualist he was one. In his personality and mannerisms there was a good deal of resemblance to Samuel Beckett, whom I remember coming to his studio. Physically they were much the same breed of man; and in Yeats's way of writing, a progress among self-generating ideas, is some resemblance to Beckett's method.

The influences on Yeats are sometimes mentioned, Daumier, for instance. I never discovered in him any interest in other painters. From a few conversations with Henry Moore, I received a very clear idea of what *he* admired in the past and of the importance he attached to the great masters. Some, he said, he could reverence without feeling that they had anything to tell him in connection with his own art. And he also said he disliked to hear people belittling the achievements of the great masters.

Yeats never talked in this way. My first recollection of hearing him discuss any painter was one day when he said he had been at a board meeting of the National Gallery at which a portrait by Tintoretto had been bought for £4,000.

He said he thought it was a waste of money. He used to give out against what he called 'brown pictures,' and might have approved of the wholesale cleaning now in vogue. He had his own ideas about everything and they were not always consistent. I'm afraid he did not appreciate Rembrandt, whom he would have included in the category of 'brown' painters; and I have a recollection of a conversation in which he dismissed Rembrandt and Tintoretto as 'journalists'. The only old master I ever heard him praise was Goya; but this was linked up with family matters, and I believe the opinion was part of his father's legacy. He said once to me that his father would have been the greatest portrait-painter since Goya if he had been content to leave alone in the afternoons what he had painted in the mornings, but a Victorian conscience made him spend the afternoon at his easel destroying the work of the morning. I took a remarkable Rowlandson cartoon to show him; and he reproached me gently. One didn't, he said, do that sort of thing. He was not offended, but he showed very little interest, and conveyed to me that I had committed a *gaffe* from inexperience.

One had to allow for a feeling of neglect; after he turned from illustrating to being a wholetime painter he did not sell a great deal. Talbot Clifton was his best patron, and there were others but, as with Hone in Yeats's youth, it was not unusual for him to take away all his larger canvases unsold from the annual exhibition of the Royal Hibernian Academy. The boom in his work coincided with the second World War. Ireland was thrown upon her own resources; there was plenty of money about and a good many parvenus. After fur coats and Chippendale chairs it became the fashion to acquire works of art. Victor Waddington took up Yeats at this time and was most successful in pushing his fortunes. Yeats had certainly very fixed ideas. He insisted that pictures should be sold according strictly to their measurements, as if they were parcels of land, and he liked them to be framed according to his own taste.

Mrs. Yeats, to whom I used to talk a great deal, made no secret of her resentment at the public's neglect of her

41

husband's oil paintings. 'If he died before me', she said once, 'I'd like to burn every picture in his studio rather than to think of them getting them'. That sounds vindictive, but it did not sound so then. I was always moved by the delight Mrs. Yeats took in her husband. They had been married for half a century; but she was as thrilled by him as if they had but lately returned from the honeymoon. I don't remember our ever talking about anything else. She said he was a very happy person and forever singing to himself. He liked to go to afternoon service at St. Patrick's to join in the hymn-singing. She felt resentment *for* him, I divined. She did not, as do so many wives, echo his opinions. She always gave me the impression that she was confiding in me. Once she took me out of the studio to show me a painting he had given her. She was as excited as a child with a wonderful new toy. She was also proud of a portrait he had painted of her (in his later manner). It was the only portrait he had ever painted, she said.

She was small and dark—rather like photographs of Katherine Mansfield (both wore their hair in a fringe). She kept herself young for his sake, I believe. As it was, she was the first to die, but not before she had the pleasure of seeing the large retrospective exhibition of her husband's painting in the National College of Art in Kildare Street. It was accompanied by every local honour and the press was uniformly enthusiastic.

It taught me one thing about Yeats, seeing his work over his lifetime. Many as its moods were, one was entirely absent. There is no hint anywhere of sensuality in Jack Yeats's paintings. His mind remained always in the condition of Robert Louis Stevenson's stories. Stevenson himself lamented that he had not broken through the convention of reticence and written more intimately about women; but I am convinced that Yeats had no desire to paint even an academic nude. He was romantic through and through, as boys are—or use to be—romantic.

There was nothing effeminate about him, nor did he suggest undue squeamishness. His personality was essentially

42

masculine but I never heard him say anything coarse; nor did he — even allowing for a reticence which a difference in age produces — ever gossip about women. A characteristic remark was a reference to an architect we both knew. 'He has that look I don't like in any man, as if he had no backside in his breeches, and was asking you not to kick him'. A well-known literary man of an earlier generation who had acquired a reputation for breaking up homes was mentioned. I think we were discussing the essence of the Don Juan character, and his name cropped up by a natural association of ideas.

'A man like that feels nothing. His aim is to perfect his art so that he has to use the least possible effort in collecting a woman. I think he has reduced it to the lifting of an eyebrow'.

W. B. Yeats was preoccupied with sex in the later years of his life; but Jack gave every appearance of being oblivious to it; and, if I were called upon to testify, my evidence would be that there had been one woman and only one in his long life.

His father had been intended for Holy Orders, but became a law student instead when Butler's *Analogies* disturbed his faith in the supernatural. And yet the older Yeats had a very reverent cast of mind. So, too, had Jack Yeats. He was particularly fond of Arnold Harvey, a near contemporary, later Bishop of Waterford, a man rather like himself in appearance, strikingly handsome in youth.

Bishop Harvey took the service at Yeats's graveside and, coming away, said to someone that Jack Yeats had been 'a very good man'. W. B. Yeats would never have inspired that remark. He looked under stones; Jack leaped over them. He said to me once (the only remark of a theological nature I can recall him making) that experience of life, if it does not teach you to believe in God, certainly convinced you of the existence of the devil. He became, so his nurse told me, increasingly distressed by the wickedness and cruelty of the world and was for ever extolling children and lamenting their inevitable involvement in the hell their elders had

43

devised. This is in keeping with my own impression that Yeats, although he liked some people more than others, was not really dependent at all on anyone's affection, although he liked attention.

In later years it was impossible to find him alone. Whenever I called I met either Victor Waddington, who confined the conversation to practical matters ('Did the electrician call? I told him to') or Tom McGreevy, Director of the National Gallery. In early days C. P. Curran was a frequent visitor to Yeats's studio. But latterly he came less, and Tom McGreevy, after Mrs. Yeats died, was in unbroken attendance. About that time Yeats used to stay in Portobello Nursing Home for the worst months of winter; and the story is probably apocryphal that a patient in a neighbouring room, not knowing McGreevy's voice, complained that Mr. Yeats kept his wireless on after midnight.

It was Tom who was largely responsible for creating the rather sycophantic air that used to prevail in the studio. He would come up to one and beg that certain topics be not mentioned as they upset Jack Yeats. English painters was one of them. When I mentioned that Francis Watson was going to give a lecture on painting of the British School, McGreevy raised his eyebrows in mock wonder. 'But what British painters *are* there?' Then he would turn to Yeats as if to acknowledge that he spoke for both of them. Yeats never said anything on these occasions. He was, I am sure, grateful for McGreevy's devotion and kindness (which were very real). But I doubt that McGreevy's championing helped Yeats's reputation. His claim in a catalogue, that Yeats was the greatest colourist to appear in Europe since Titian, aroused the ire of critics in England, who hit back as critics do when claims of that order provoke them.

About that preface I have cause to feel ashamed because McGreevy handed it to me and later asked me what I thought of his essay. I said something encouraging, evasive and insincere (because I never paid very much attention to McGreevy's critical opinions). Afterwards when I saw the hostility his writing evoked I was very sorry that I hadn't

44

read it and at least put in a word of caution; but McGreevy would hardly have agreed to tone his praises down.

Greatly though I liked Yeats as a man, more than any older man I have ever known, and substantial as the pleasure his painting and drawing have given me, I must confess to an inability to appreciate either his books or his plays. He put his dreams and his poetry into his true art. The discipline lent them force. In writing and speech I though he was self-indulgent and incoherent.

This inability was the cause of embarrassment when his play *In Sand* was produced at the Peacock Theatre. It was a great occasion, but I found the play essentially undramatic. One character sat on the stage and spoke a monologue that seemed to go on for half-an-hour. I did not see in Yeats any of the characteristics of the dramatist, although he could do or say nothing to which he didn't lend some of his own antiseptic charm. I knew that Yeats set great store by the success of the play and I had the usual struggle as to what to write to him afterwards. Between the claims of friendship, fellow-feeling, the desire to please and not to wound and the claims of integrity it is not always easy to strike a satisfactory balance. Whatever I wrote was greeted, so McGreevy informed me, with the remark, 'Well, there is after all a great deal to be said for courtesy'. But on a subsequent evening in the studio I listened to McGreevy retailing the remarks of various members of the audience. Few, it may be said, who knew Dublin would fail to know that Yeats would in all probability hear what they had to say. Yeats made no effort to hide his displeasure with praise that carried any qualification. Lennox Robinson was the enemy in chief. Yeats did not like him; this may have been tied up with Yeats's ambitions as a playwright. Robinson had sufficient influence in the Abbey to get plays performed there, and this he did not do for Yeats.

W. B. Yeats's plays never attracted much of an audience; and there were constant complaints by Austin Clarke and others that the Abbey neglected verse plays. The trouble was, and is, that few people enjoy them unless they are by

Shakespeare. Jack Yeats very rarely showed any such anxiety about what people thought of his paintings. He certainly never abused anyone for neglecting them; but he did show himself vitally concerned about the fortunes of his plays.

We once went together to a play in the Gaiety. We sat in the front row because Yeats said he found it hard to hear. Neither of us enjoyed it; I can remember him saying, 'When I saw the piano on the set, I knew what we were in for. You can always tell when a piano is one of the props. The heroine will play it in the last act'. None of the Yeats family of that generation had an ear for music. Yeats said to me once that he disapproved of a dramatist taking an active interest music. 'When I see a piano in the studio I know that the worst has happened'.

R. R. Figgis told me a story about Yeats which is revealing. He was invited to a luncheon with C. P. Curran and others given in honour of someone who was lecturing to the Royal Dublin Society. The conversation was of an improving sort; and Yeats kept quiet. Suddenly, he broke out. 'Cezanne, Cezanne, Cezanne. Sez you'. He himself never talked in a learned way, never discussed literature, and, I suspect, preferred to read Mark Twain or Bret Harte or perhaps Jack London. He gave me two books from his shelves. They were reminiscences of a sort still to be discovered in secondhand bookstalls, with such chapter-headings as 'Australian Days', 'Back in Fleet Street Again.' I accepted them as gestures of friendship; but I could never unravel the impulse that prompted the selection.

Tragedy sometimes made an appearance in Yeats's paintings of later years. There is a large one which shows a figure on the ground and another standing over it called 'Death for One Only'. I have heard this described as if it referred to the death of W.B. leaving Jack to carry on the family tradition. I doubt this. After the death of his father his paintings show no indication of sadness and I believe his father meant more to Yeats that his brother did. Elton describes the old man's attitude to the English, for example, 'He was ever ready to hold forth on "the Englishman", a theme that was to pervade his letters from overseas. *The Englishman*, in his eyes, came to be a type (Tory, class-proud, official, public schoolboy, self-centred, etc.) but he made many a concession to our poetry and to our common people'.

That might read as a description of Jack Yeats's idiosyncratic attitude; and he inherited it clearly from his father's table-talk, to which he listened. If he was less often with him, he probably took all the keener an impression of those dissertations.

A wife's attitude is not evidence of her husband's opinions, or I should say that Jack Yeats behind his brother got an unfair share of recognition. The poet won his reputation as a lyric poet in England. He was awarded a Civil List pension (so was Lady Wilde; both were ferocious rebels on paper). Jack Yeats was known in Ireland for his drawings and broadsheet illustrations; and in England he had made an impression with comic drawings — but this was not fame, much less the sort he wanted.

I have said that Mrs. Yeats spoke bitterly of public neglect of her husband. His fame came with the discovery of his work by the Irish during the war years. The rest of his life was a campaign to establish in England the position to which Clark's National Gallery exhibition gave a foothold. The English critics refused to be bowled over, or to give Yeats the place according to, say, Sickert or Matthew Smith. Lowry, a regional artist, is nearer the mark. Yeats was stamped with the stigma of regionalism, that is to say of having a less than universal appeal. It is borne out by Clark's assertion that he never thinned his art for export but preserved the native flavour. This was generally recognised, but the implication of the bulk of criticism was that he didn't because he couldn't. It was almost as if the English critics were fighting against Jack's traditional disparagement of England and things English, as if they saw in his fidelity to his own myths a refusal to recognise their standards, a refusal based on inability to do other than he did. His technical skill is no business of mine here; but his

47

reputation will, I surmise, ultimately depend not on that but on the poetry which he conveyed in a personal way in paint. His painting by that contention depended on the poetry; and his chances of mortality, therefore, will depend on the quality of that poetry. It is limited but strong; limitation can be a source of strength. Beside one of Jack Yeats's evocations of an Irish landscape, especially when he introduces a horse or one of his fantasy figures, a conventional landscape looks timid in comparison.

Most people outgrow their youth; Yeats remained close to his childhood in Sligo. The theme reappeared endlessly in his paintings. For a time the Irish troubles made a mark; then, I would say — on the evidence of the paintings alone — that the death of Mrs. Yeats was reflected in at least one painting, 'The Great Tent is down', which shows stragglers going home and deserting the field; a pole stands where, earlier, the tent spread its canvas. I remember looking at it in the company of Richard McGonigal, who made a good collection of Yeats's paintings. We were alone for a moment; Yeats must have gone out of the studio to find an orange in the kitchen (he attached a special ceremony to the handing round of sherry and always put in a sliced orange peel. He himself drank whiskey). We were both overwhelmed by the painting; but McGonigal said 'I couldn't live with it. It's too tragic'.

That was some months after Mrs. Yeats died. Around that time I saw more of him that I was to do in the last years when MacGreevy or Victor Waddington was present when I called and gave the conversation their respective tones. We dined together during the weeks when Mrs. Yeats was dying, and it seemed quite natural to call on him one morning after she died, although as a rule, I would not have dreamt of invading the studio until the end of the day.

I found Yeats at breakfast; it was a beautiful morning; the sun came into the room lighting up a picture I had never seen before. It shows a stevedore coming up from a harbour, passing the open door of a forge. We talked and then Yeats went out of the room and came back and said, without any show of emotion: 'Cottie never made a will, but I know what she wanted me to do, and she would have liked you to have that as a little remembrance'. He handed me a cheque for £100. I had been praising the new picture to him; and, on an impulse, I asked if he would allow me to use the legacy to buy it. He seemed to be pleased; and I have as a result a special feeling about that Yeats. It is its lovely self and a part of our friendship.

About that time I had discovered the novels of Elizabeth Bowen and I used to meet her with several friends we had in common. With the best of intentions I hoped to bring Elizabeth Bowen and Jack Yeats together. We had been to see his retrospective exhibition together and afterwards we dined and called on Yeats in his studio after dinner. Conversation was constrained. Perhaps she didn't really care for his pictures. Yeats thought she was under the impression he expected her to buy one and launched forth on a Yeats treatise about the English who settled in Cork and never realised that they were living in Ireland or became Irish.

He was never at a loss. One night he came with me to a Christmas dinner of the 'Strollers', a musical dining club. There must have been over two hundred people present. Dr. Kirkpatrick, who presided, called on Yeats to reply to the toast of the guests. He had given him no warning; it was a large gathering with none of the comfort of an impromptu speaker can find on an informal occasion with a group of friends, and Yeats was then past eighty. He seemed to pale, then rose to his feet, and for exactly the right length of time made a wholly appropriate happy speech. That night he made a suggestion, which I found in one of his books in another connection, that Government should alter income-tax to a tax on personal beauty. Everyone would then seek to pay as much as possible and proudly exhibit the most crippling assessments.

Yeats was himself incapable of wounding and devoid of arrogance (W.B. was not) and as he grew older became increasingly insistent on the need for kindness. He valued goodness in people. It is a quality of which it is no longer fashionable to speak. As faith in its ultimate reward has come to be shaken; 'Compassion', 'justice'—behaviour that affects people as groups in ways that can be recorded in statistics—are now more popular than personal merit. A man who makes his own family miserable is never deterred from prescribing for the happiness of the world or diffident about taking on its regeneration because he has been a failure in his own home and unable to fulfil his personal obligations.

To this new ethos Yeats was averse. His idea of goodness was personal, goodness of the old-fashioned sort. It required us to be kind and self-effacing and chivalrous in our own lives; and that is exactly what he was as a man.

AN INTERVIEW
WITH JACK BUTLER YEATS[1]

by Shotaro Oshima

Jack Butler Yeats, younger brother of W. B. Yeats, was a noted painter and a member of the Royal Hibernian Academy. He received the honorary degrees of LL.D. from Dublin University and of D.Litt. from the National University of Ireland. A few years before his death, in the spring of 1955, he held a one-man exhibition at the Victor Waddington Galleries, thus giving proof of his excellent poetic imagination.

On January 26, 1956, he sent me a letter, in which he wrote that he had had the year of his birth taken out of any biographical dictionary, for he had believed for a long time that 'a creative artist should not be valued because of his age and that such an artist should leave his age as vague as possible'. And so while he was alive I never knew how old he was, but on his death on March 28, 1957, *The Irish Times* reported in the outlines of his career that he was born in 1871. And I then found out for the first time that he had lived more than eighty-six years.

It was on July 7, 1938, that I visited him. I was caught in heavy rain on the way, and at four o'clock in the afternoon I knocked at the door of his house in Fitzwilliam Square, Dublin, with my dripping hat drawn down over my eyes. The artist who received me warmly looked taller and more slender than his brother. He was long-faced and his thin hair hung about his forehead.

After he had talked on various subjects, I said, 'You have often chosen typically Irish scenes. Would you kindly show me some of your paintings?'

'While young, I painted a number of pictures representing

[1] From *Yeats and Japan* (Tokyo 1965).

typically Irish scenes and people living in those scenes. Would you care to come to my studio upstairs?' I followed him upstairs, hearing the sound of rain pattering on the roof and the window.

'I have just been to Scotland and seen the desolate landscapes of mountains there'. I said after we had seated ourselves, 'and it's a great pleasure for me now to see pictures of Irish landscapes and Irish folk'.

'This picture represents the gloomy houses of poor people in Dublin. That is a public house where the tenants of tenement houses gather. In that picture I tried to paint a port in Kerry full of cargo boats. This is a scene in the countryside of Galway. My brother William once lived here with his family. This is a shore landscape in the south-east part of Ireland. That picture in the corner represents O'Connell Bridge. You must have crossed it several times'. With these words of explanation he moved his right hand busily as if he were painting a picture.

'What I feel from these pictures is that your style of painting is realistic when you choose natural scenes, while in such subjects as the life of poor Dubliners, the scene of a port town and labourers in the street you become rather an impressionist'. Looking at his paintings, I was fascinated by the green, undulating hills, the smooth and extensive surface of a lake, the fleecy clouds floating in the azure sky, the white surf booming upon a rocky shore; all typically Irish and painted with a delicate touch.

'My style has changed recently. You have been to Rosses Point, I think. The picture which was titled "Memory Harbour" and used as a frontispiece to my brother's *Reveries over Childhood and Youth* represents the harbour in that village. At that time I intended to be a realist'.

'Do you mean that you are no longer a realist? But I found much poetic vision in that picture'.

'Art flows on incessantly and changes all the time. Things in the external world may seem always the same to some people, but an artist finds them different when a change is brought about in him. He must not try to go against this

52

inner change. There are many pictures of mine exhibited in the Municipal Gallery of Dublin. He showed me one of his pictures as an example of how the artist struggles on with the power and freedom of mind, and cherishes a sharper passion in form and newer movement in design'.

I gazed at the picture he had indicated. There were two travellers painted on the canvas, one of whom was hovering between life and death. Dark clouds hung over the wilderness. The dying man seemed to be struggling with the agony of death, his muscles quivering convulsively.

'This dying man's body seems to be a lump of clay rather than a human body,' I said. 'Does the glimmer of his body express the intense agony he is struggling with? The other man standing by his side looks like a ghost. He looks as if a shrivelled tree loomed in the dark'.

'Yes; the skin of the dying man has become inflamed and he appears to be in his last agony. This man, also, once walked proudly and elatedly'.

The rain was falling incessantly outside. The verdure of the leaves seen through the window looked all the more fresh in the rain. Jack rose to his feet and tried to pull out a larger piece from a bundle of pictures propped up against the wall near the window. It was very large, but with my help he just managed to pull it out. It was five feet wide and four feet tall, and was titled 'Helen of Troy.'

'This is a product of my fancy,' he said. 'It is based on the legend that Helen's beauty launched a thousand ships.'

'What a tremendous picture this is! It reminds me of some pictures of supernatural beauty painted by Blake.'

'You see Helen dancing in a boat in the middle of the picture. Her golden hair is flowing like a flame to suggest her burning passion. The graceful curve of her body shows that she is dancing. At her feet crouches a figure, half brute and half human, with fixed eyes. It is recording the names of all the ships that are going down to the bottom. The background of these two figures is, of course, formed by innumerable ships.'

'I see the clouds are sweeping across the sky and the ships

53

are in array in the terrible lightning. They are doomed to sink in the mixture of light and shade, aren't they?'

'I tried to express a truth deeper than a mere fact. I have little knowledge of Greek, but this monster is meant to be writing down the names of the ships in Greek.'

He smiled. He was so intent on what he was saying that he did not notice that the kettle he had put over the fire to serve tea was boiling over. So I ran to the fireplace and removed the lid of the kettle.

'Ah! the water was boiling over? Thank you,' he said, turning to me from the picture.

'I think there is much difference between your earlier realistic works and your recent ones, especially such experimental pieces as this.'

'Every artist, if he deserves that name, must necessarily change. Perhaps you know James Joyce's style. It is natural that an artist should change incessantly in his style like Joyce. It is an inevitable process. Compare, for example, Joyce's *Anna Livia Plurabelle* with his earlier works. You will see how great the difference is. You had better see Joyce. He stays in France now, and he will be glad to see you. He writes tremendously big letters, for he cannot see well. (So saying he drew some letters as big as his hand in the air.) He now dictates his works to a copyist he has employed. There is an interesting episode about that. One day he was dictating to the copyist as usual, when there was a knock at the door. Joyce said, "Come in!" and the copyist wrote down "Come in!" The next day when Joyce was listening to the copyist reading the manuscript he had dictated, he was surprised to hear the words "Come in!" in an unexpected place. He said to the copyist that he couldn't have dictated such words. The copyist answered that he had certainly heard them. Joyce laughted and said "Ah! I remember. Please leave the words as they are. I said those words to the knocking at the door. Don't cross them out. There is some meaning even in words uttered casually." ' Jack ended this episode with a hearty laugh, and added, 'There may be some people who will laugh at such a piece as mine as the product of

54

mere phantasy. But even in mere phantasy there often are things inseparable from truth, or things more real than reality itself. It is the very world a true artist lives in.'

The reader may judge from the conversation I recorded above that Jack was a very eloquent person. But the impression he made on me was that there could be few people so modest, so naïve, so shy and so amiable. I found in this quiet-mannered gentleman a true artist who, faithful to his imagination, would never stop painting till his last day — a typical Irishman. He seemed even more careless about his appearance than his brother. Seeing his necktie loose and crooked I was the more attracted to him.

Then he gave me a book of his dramas. It was entitled *Apparition,* and contained ' The Old Sea Road' and 'Rattle' besides a piece with the same title as the book.

'This book was published in 1933,' he said, 'I meant it to be performed on a stage surrounded by the audience. In the middle of the stage is an oval table, on which is an inkstand. Seven chairs are placed around the table. It is a coffee room in a hotel. I wanted to make an experiment when I attached such stage directions to the play. But there is no one who will put such an experimental piece on the stage. Such a play is not fit for the stage in Ireland, to say nothing of England. By the way, have you been to the Abbey Theatre to see Shaw's play?'

'Yes; I saw his "Millionairess" last night. It was too verbose for me to enjoy.'

'I saw the play with my wife. Mr. Shaw takes every opportunity to advertise his works. His publishers avail themselves of this habit of his and can sell his books with little advertising expense. But he will not let the publishers gain a big profit, for he demands a high royalty on his books. Then he has constant readers among ladies.'

'Besides Shaw, who are the popular playwrights in Ireland? Do your dramas sell well?'

'Even my pictures have almost no demand, still less my dramas. In America there are many social organizations created by plutocrats such as Carnegie or the Rockefeller

Foundation, and artists receive considerable benefit. But in Dublin we can find few people who will buy our pictures. Almost all the great works in the Municipal Gallery were donated by the painters themselves. I exhort you to visit the Gallery by all means, for you will find there many pictures representing typically Irish landscapes and people.' While he was talking, the rain became heavier and poured down violently.

'I'm going to visit your sister, Miss Corbet Yeats, to-morrow morning. I'm very glad to have seen you and have enjoyed the afternoon very much.'

'Then I will phone my sister and inform her of your visit. Shall I call a taxi?'

'Oh, no! thank you!'

The rain was still falling when I said good-bye to the painter. The little square where we stood presented a lonely and deserted appearance. He shook me warmly by the hand, asking me to revisit Dublin and see him again. After he had entered the house, I stood alone on the pavement of the square and looked up at the lighted window of his studio. It was the only light in Fitzwilliam Square. In the steady fall of rain I left the place, picturing to myself the figure of the artist sitting alone among images of his own creation.

SIX DRAWINGS BY JACK B. YEATS

for A LAMENT FOR ART O'LEARY

Frank O'Connor's translation of 'A Lament for Art O'Leary' from the Irish of Eibhlín Dubh Ní Chonaill was first printed in his collection *Lords and Commons,* issued by the Cuala Press in an edition of two hundred and fifty copies in the autumn of 1938, a book which went to press immediately after the completion of the 1937 series of *A Broadside,* edited by W. B. Yeats and Dorothy Wellesley, for which Jack B. Yeats had made a number of drawings.

His return to the Cuala Press in the 1930's was a happy one for Jack B. Yeats and resulted in his finest work for the Cuala Press, completed in 1940, the illustrated edition of *A Lament for Art O'Leary.* For this book a large quarto format was chosen, allowing the drawings generous margin and each of the six drawings in the book was coloured by hand. The edition was limited to one hundred and thirty copies only and is today a rare collector's piece. A facsimile of the hand coloured edition is being issued by the Irish University Press, but, by permission of the Directors of the Cuala Press, the original black and white versions of the six Jack B. Yeats drawings are here shown for the first time.

LIAM MILLER.

THE PAINTINGS OF JACK B. YEATS[1]

by Ernie O'Malley

Jack B. Yeats spent his boyhood in Sligo town, a small port on the Atlantic edge. Sligo is flanked in a half-circle by mountains which show a wild inland cliff scenery shaped to fantastic form; small lakes, then strong outbursts of rock carry the other flank to the sea. The sea brought the outside world to the doors of a small town in a casual mention of foreign cities, strange words and wild doings; it made for wonder and mystery later seen if only as a gloss on piracy. From the land side came the country people to shop, shy and awkward in the foreign life of a town, but fierce and intractable when following their realistic land calling at fairs and markets. Family life for them centred around the oldest of man's allegiances, the hearth, woven with memoried legend; their land work built as much on folklore as on the hard reality of uneconomic holdings.

The town presented a knoweldge of character and incident, the vagaries of personalities with oddities even to the daft accepted as part of its world. It would be an open book like any other Irish town, whose inhabitants are mainly interested in motive and intention of others, in knitting daily events in a conversational form to be related before evening as direct and indirect implication threaded by affection, malice or envy.

Here then in his native town he could see people who were not accepted in a conventional setting. They bore much the same relationship to the tightened security of bourgeois respectability, ringed by experience which it fears to enlarge, as the artist does to that life; and with them the unexpected was always in the offing. The sailor, a transitory form who came on shore for drink and company after the indifference

1 Introduction to the catalogue of the Exhibition of Paintings by Jack B. Yeats, Dublin 1945.

of ocean, forgetful of hardship in his now remembrance of outland ways and customs, to light the imagination of stay-at-homes. Tinkers with the wildness of life in the open and their utterly untamed fierceness who fought after a feed of porter in a whoop of song. Countrymen, freed for a few days in the year from the greedy tyranny of land, wander through their favourite pubs to meet neighbours and relations, ridding themselves of hard-earned money in a spacious generosity; at ease in gestured extravagance with a background of their own song. Outside in the street a ballad singer to relate past and present in a long string of verse, sure of heightened talk and soothing drink before the night came.

When the circus arrived its flamboyant posters exalted grace and beauty to ballet level, a band renowned for noise shook the side walls whilst brightly costumed performers wound through the streets. At night, clowns in their tragic way acted the scapegoat, slapped their fellows, made fun of themselves in simulated awkwardness, often to emerge from this chrysalis, as grace. The clown related his humour to the tragic scene of life inherent in his audience, though outsiders, as in the clown, might see only uncaring lightheartedness. Circus music, colour, baroque gesture, essentially sweep the mind, free the heart, but relate nomadic tent existence to settlement, leaving an aching sense of unfulfilment and nostalgia behind.

Jack Yeats would be moulded too by the physical nature of his province, Connacht. Great roaring winds sweep in from the Atlantic to drench the land with spray, soften the intention, weaken will and perseverance. Cloud forms drift slowly in threat or, when storm has ceased, model to a painter's delight land forms below. Sky bulks large to give a sense of infinite distance and mystery mixed with tragic desolation. This spaciousness of sky is the most noticeable feature of the Western scene; it is, at times, as if the land were a prelude to the atmosphere above. Swirling cloud makes for a Turneresque dramatic effect, difficult to register, shot as it is with daffodil, duck-egg green and improbable

65

colour combinations. Land can become sogged with persistent rain; it is then more than ever a burden and a heartbreaking task to work, or to brood a melancholy in the mind. With shafted light after the rain comes a lyrical mood in which tender greens vibrate in tones, whins crash with yellow glory and atmosphere is radiant.

The shifting scene is temperamental and induces mood. It is a hard country to paint as it presents problems of subtle, unrelated colour which is not easily seen as pattern, but develops in a strange orchestration. This subtlety and its opposite, the strongly dramatic scene, must be the despair of academic painters whose minds have been trained to accept the conventional impression, but whose eye may fail to record the sudden unexpected impact. Memory must play its part, for painting hours are episodic, broken by rain or rebellious wind. The sense of man is present in enclosures of light-filigreed stone walls which map land hunger, or in unobtrusive cottages, dwarfed by mountain and hill to an almost tragic insignificance.

Beyond the Shannon in a train the West can be sensed: in a spate of talk, an expansion of interest which breaks down impersonal aloofness to introduce the co-operative sharing of a sense of life, an immediate hint of vitality and a degree of wonder which rounds a mediaeval quality of mind. People have charm, time is judged as a convenience not as a burden, talk is an expression in a form of entertainment which interests to free the imagination and give a sense of ease. Subtlety of mind, easily directed to cunning in land or business, is now judged as diplomatic adroitness. Above all is a sense of wildness and freedom, an untamed naturalness, the unexpected even in a phrase, a feeling of equality through an understanding of the natural dignity of man.

Jack Yeats experienced some such quality of life in Connacht and he has since interpreted it. With a hawk's swift eye he has seen this panorama as material, and his sensitive psychological understanding of it has fused its meaning in his spirit. The visual world has been absorbed, selected and recreated slowly with innocent freshness in terms of emotional

66

colour. He can capture the intensity of his feeling which has viewed an aspect of as simple a pleasure of life as the interior of a circus tent. The circus is a boy's delight but also a man's, if his emotions have not been smothered by what is known as discretion, or by the death of the heart.

There is a genuine interest and affection in his work for the incidents portrayed. They grow out of love and a profound sensibility of what to some are outlandish ways with a certain colourful appeal. The outward form of life has changed since he has grown up but the fundamental attitude of mind remains. Practical people often find life in the West hard; as indeed it is when progress is viewed philosophically in relation to eternity; but artists whose energy is turned to observation see the relationship of people to each other, to events and to their environment.

In his earlier work he is a draughtsman who stresses illustrative content directing it in a *vital* sense of line to a personal idiom. Later, in water-colour he uses water-colour with this same illustrative content not as a medium but as flat colour tones to give vitality to his drawings. It was, I think, a lucky chance when he found a number of his early water-colours destroyed by damp. This accident made him think more in terms of oil and he began to experiment. Then continued a long period in which definition became gradually more colourful and his essential bent, that of a colourist, more emphatic. By the year 1921 he had reached the limits of his expression in this manner.

When the artist reaches his spiritual limit in any one method of expression he follows either of two ways. He continues to reproduce his impressions in a manner he has outgrown until the individual painting is no longer a problem for the sum total of what constitutes his being, but is related to hand and eye alone: or he experiments until he has created a new way of approach to his problem. Jack Yeats found his world in a greater feeling for the emotional use of paint, which slowly pushed back the limits of definition until paint, as it were, escaped its mould to became an end in itself. It is hard to explain a change in direction, but one of the factors may have been the heightened sensibility which could result from the tension of life during the struggle for freedom in Ireland then, and the new note of intensity felt by a sensitive observer.

As he enlarged his experience as a painter, he also enlarged his vision. His work no longer dealt with a perception of countrymen in relaxation or at ease in a folk-lore tradition. His figures now enter a subjective world in which they are related to the loneliness of the individual soul, the vague lack of pattern in living with its sense of inherent tragedy, brooding nostalgia, associated with time as well as variation on the freer moments as of old. Visionary worlds of Tir-na-nOg, California, palaces, are opened to us with persuasive paint, and all action is subordinated to thought. Aspects of Dublin workers are searched for inherent character or nobility. Anna Liffey gets its due tribute from one who has the Dubliner's realisation of its significance; reflective mood floods people and furniture in light-splashed rooms; or light itself is the subtly dramatic force. He had always a strong sense of man in relation to the impersonality of the Irish scene; isolated figures never dominate the landscape, but they are now more related to it in symbolical significance which increases their stature to bulk in the mind. One departure of his was completely new in Irish painting, the depiction of national events. The memory of the dead makes for a tragic understanding in Ireland. It evokes a feeling of dead generations who served or had died for a common cause, their struggle echoed in each generation. The Bachelor's Walk incident is shown as a simple, but hieratic incident of a flower-girl who casts a flower outside a doorway where men have been shot down. There is restrained dignity and grace in the movement of her hand and a tenderness that evokes a sense of pity.

He has used the funeral or burial as a symbol. The death of a man who has suffered in the national fight has often been one of the few public tributes that a people could give to one whom some of them recognised only by death. A sense of ceremonial, which had seemed to disappear from consciousness, would emerge and an impressive ordered intensity shows understanding and devotion. The memory of the dead has changed its meaning when seen as a political artifice, or has become outworn in verbal misuse, but in Jack Yeats's pictures it holds an eternal significance.

For over twenty years he has been painting in this new manner. For a time he worked in philosophic isolation amongst an indifferent audience who resent an artist's new direction in implementing his vision. This has always been the attitude of a world of punditry, which, becoming complacent, does not risk disturbance except in terms of what it regards as its own interpretation of creative work. A true artist's vision is directed by a keener mental and physical eye, trained selective capacity, contemplative detachment, and inventive technical sense, which is used to rebuild the microcosm architecturally, descriptively, or emotionally. Gradually, however, people came to recognise his genius and originality, his unusual colour sense and his absolute integrity. Of late he has himself been the major factor in the training of our eyes to understand what is indeed a school in itself, his quality of mind in paint.

In Ireland the visual sense is not strongly developed in terms of creative painting, but there is a fine feeling for colour, well expressed in small towns where white-wash is mixed with paint powder to give house fronts a fascinating texture of tender pastel shades. Irish atmosphere softens and blends the clash that might have ensued from the individuality of the owners in selection of colour. There is, as well, a peculiar unliterary affection of landscape, but the manner of looking at paint is too often determined, not by this corrective, based as it is on evasive colour and the inherent structural sense of line and form in bare mountain, but by thinking of other paintings. Due to the destruction of the arts by conquest there is but one continuous tradition, the literary tradition; we are inclined to see paint in a literary way as if the implied title should continue as a story on the canvas.

In Jack Yeats we have a painter who is as much concerned with what he has to say in paint as with his manner of saying it. He brings a fresh experience to each canvas he paints; his

69

individual work can not be judged in terms of previous work but in the individual canvas one looks at. That demands alertness of mind and an unprejudiced, innocent eye. He is a romantic painter who through memory had made notes all his life of material which has stirred him by its emotional significance. Those notes may remain unused for years but they have been sifted in his conscousness. When he calls on them he can recollect his original impressions, organise his perceptions through an enlargement of that experience, and create a work of art.

With him colour is an emotional force and his method of using it varies in regard to its substance as pigment and as texture. He may create a homogeneous surface with his brush, improvise an absorbing study in chiaroscuro, or use the priming of the canvas to aid luminosity of light and shade. At times, impatient with the brush to communicate his feeling for the richness and charm of pigment and his sheer joy of its expressive power, he employs the palette knife to give swiftness and vigour to the immediacy of his emotion. Seemingly unrelated colours directed by this urgency create an orchestration due to his unerring taste in colour harmony; and in a form of evocative magic, make a direct impact on the mind. Even a casual glance at a small collection of his work shows how inexhaustible is his colour invention. As he experiments in technique he reaches a point in mastery where his handling of knife or brush seems to be by instinct.

In this exhibition as his development is studied from his earlier stages to his more subjective and symbolical work, his steady growth can be seen. The new Ireland, still fluid politically and socially, has found in Jack Yeats a painter of major rank, whose vision is used to make us aware of inherent characteristics, psychological directives and eternal verities.

In return for this understanding of us it is pleasant to realise that Irish art lovers should, over the years, have made it possible to bring together a collection of his pictures that show his development in its completeness, and thus bring about the present tribute from the whole nation.

70

TWO PIECES BY SAMUEL BECKETT

Thomas MacGreevy, one of the first art critics to appreciate the greatness of Jack B. Yeats, wrote a short study, *Jack B. Yeats: an appreciation and an interpretation,* about 1937, but could find no publisher for it. It was published by the Three Candles Press, Dublin, in 1945, with a postscript in which MacGreevy surveyed the development of Yeats's art during the intervening period.

MacGreevy saw Yeats fundamentally as a humanist who found his real subject in Ireland and who expressed the Ireland that matters, the 'Ireland that has a heart', and her people, who in the twentieth century had a fresh opportunity to develop their humanity and to give it imaginative expression. He identified the painters with what was best in the nation's struggle for identity. Samuel Beckett's review of the book relates Yeats's work to the miraculous disaster of existence.

The second piece, published nine years later, was Mr. Beckett's contribution to a symposium of French critical views of an exhibition of Jack B. Yeats's work.

R. McH.

MacGREEVY ON YEATS [1]

by Samuel Beckett

This is the earliest connected account of Mr. Yeats's painting. To it future writers on the subject will, perhaps, be indebted, no less than writers on Proust to Madariaga's essay, or writers on Joyce to Curtius's — indebted for an attitude to develop, or correct, or reject. It is rare for the first major reaction to art of genius to come, as here, from a compatriot of the artist. The causes of this are no doubt profound and forcible. It is agreeable to find them coerced.

The greater part of this essay was written in London, in 1938. A postscript, written this year in Ireland, covers Mr. Yeats's development from 1938 to the present day. The past

---

[1] *The Irish Times,* 4 August 1945.

seven years have confirmed Mr. MacGreevy in the views
that a dozen London publishers, not yet so fortunate as to
lack paper, declined to publish. This is not to be wondered
at. It is difficult to formulate what it is one likes in Mr.
Yeats's painting, or indeed what it is one likes in anything,
but it is a labour not easily lost, and a relationship once
started not likely to fail, between such a knower and such an
unknown.

There is at least this to be said for mind, that it can dispel
mind. And at least this for art-criticism, that it can lift from
the eyes, before *rigor vitae* sets in, some of the weight of con-
genital prejudice. Mr. MacGreevy's little book does this
with a competence that will not surprise those who have read
his essay on Mr. Eliot, or his admirable translation of
Valéry's *Introduction à la Méthode de Léonard de Vinci,*
nor those who follow, in the *Record,* his articles on writers
and artists little known, as yet, in the Republic.

THE NATIONAL PAINTER

Mr. MacGreevy sees in Mr. Yeats the first great painter, the
first great Irish painter, that Ireland has produced, or indeed,
could have produced; the first to fix, plastically, with completeness and for his time finality, what is peculiar to the
Irish scene and to the Irish people. This is the essence of his
interpretation, and it permeates the essay in all its parts.
The position is made clear at the outset:

. . . What was unique in Ireland was that the life of the
people considered itself, and was in fact, spiritually and
culturally as well as politically, the whole life of the
nation. Those who acted for the nation officially were
outside the nation. They had a stronger sense of identity
with the English governing class than with the people of
Ireland, and their art was no more than a province of
English art. The first genuine artist, therefore, who so
identified himself with the people of Ireland as to be able
to give true and good and beautiful artistic expression to
the life they lived, and to that sense of themselves as the
Irish nation, inevitably became not merely a *genre* painter
like the painters of the *petit peuple* in other countries, and

72

not merely a nation's painter in the sense of Pol de Limbourg, Louis Le Nian, Bassano, Ostade or Jan Steen were national painters, but *the* national painter in the sense that Rembrandt and Velasquez and Watteau were national painters, the painter who in his work was the consummate expression of the spirit of his own nation at one of the supreme points in its evolution.

This, the Constable and Watteau analogies, the statement of the political backgrounds to the first (until about 1923) and the second periods, the elucidations of 'Helen' and 'The Blood of Abel', seem to me art-criticism of a high order, indeed. They constitute an affirmation of capital importance, not only for those who feel in this way about Mr. Yeats, or for those who as yet feel little or nothing about Mr. Yeats, but also for those, such as myself, who feel in quite a different way about Mr. Yeats.

THE ARTIST

The national aspects of Mr. Yeats's genius have, I think, been over-stated, and for motives not always remarkable for their aesthetic purity. To admire painting on other than aesthetic grounds, or a painter, *qua* painter, for any other reason than that he is a good painter, may seem to some uncalled for. And to some also it may seem that Mr. Yeats's importance is to be sought elsewhere than in a sympathetic treatment (how sympathetic?) of the local accident, or the local substance. He is with the great of our time, Kandinsky and Klee, Ballmer and Bram van Velde, Rouault and Braque, because he brings light, as only the great dare to bring light, to the issueless predicament of existence, reduces the dark where there might have been, mathematically at least, a door. The being in the street, when it happens in the room, the being in the room when it happens in the street, the turning to gaze from land to sea, from sea to land, the backs to one another and the eyes abandoning, the man alone trudging in sand, the man alone thinking (thinking!) in his box — these are characteristic notations having reference, I imagine, to processes less simple, and less delicious, than those to which

73

the plastic *vis* is commonly reduced, and to a world where Tir-na-nOgue makes no more sense than Bachelor's Walk, nor Helen than the apple-woman, nor asses than men, nor Abel's blood than Useful's, nor morning than night, nor inward than the outward search.

HOMMAGE A JACK B. YEATS [1]

by Samuel Beckett

Ce qu'a d'icomparable cette grande oeuvre solitaire est son insistance à renvoyer au plus secret de l'esprit qui la souleve et à ne se laisser éclairer qu'au jour de celui-ci.

Da là cette étrangeté sans example et que laissent entière les habituels recours aux patrimoines, national et autres. Quoi de moins féerique que cette prestigieuse facture comme soufflée par la chose à faire, et par son urgence propre? Quant aux repondants qu'on a bien fini par lui dénicher, Ensor et Munch en tête, le moins qu'on puisse en dire est qu'ils ne nous sont pas d'un grand secours.

L'artiste qui joue son être est de nulle part. Et il n'a pas de frères.

Broder alors? Sur ces images éperdument immédiates il n'y a ni place, ni temps, pour les exploits rassurants. Sur cette violence de besoin qui now seulement les déchaîne, mais les bouleverse jusqu'au delà de leur horizons. Sur ce grand réel intérieur où fantômes morts et vivants, nature et vide, tout ce qui n'a de cesse et tout ce qui ne sera jamais, s'intègrent en une seule évidence et pour une seule déposition.

Enfin sur cette suprême maîtrise qui se soumet à l'immaîtrisable, et tremble.

Non.

S'incliner simplement, émerveillé.

HOMAGE TO JACK B. YEATS *by* Samuel Beckett.

Translated by Ruby Cohn

What is incomparable in this great solitary *oeuvre* is its insistence upon sending us back to the darkest part of the spirit that created it and upon permitting illuminations only through that darkness.

Hence this unparallelled strangeness which renders irrelevant the usual tracing of a heritage, whether national or other.

---

[1] *Les Lettres Nouvelles,* April, 1954.

What is less magic than this extraordinary craftsmanship, as if inspired by the thing to be done in its own urgency?

As for references that have been unearthed — Ensor and Munch at the top of the list — the least that can be said is that they are not much help.

The artist who stakes his being comes from nowhere. And he has no brothers.

Shall I embellish? There is neither place nor time for reassuring notes on these desperately immediate images. On this violence of need which not only unleashes them but disrupts them beyond their vanishing lines. On this great internal reality which incorporates into a single witness dead and living spirits, nature and void, everything that will cease and everything that will never be. And finally on this supreme master who submits to what cannot be mastered, and trembles.

No.

One can simply bow, wonder-struck.

JACK B. YEATS:
PROMISE AND REGRET

by Brian O'Doherty

'The true painter must be part of the land and of the life he paints.'
'An artist should avoid conventions, even if the conventions are his own invention.'

JACK B. YEATS.

I

Jack B. Yeats is dangerous for an Irishman to write about. He presents to the Irish mind 'verities' it would be unpatriotic, indeed immoral, to question or reject. Yeats tapped the energies of a mythological monster ('Ireland'— itself a one-word poem); in writing about him is one engaging in a kind of quixotic mission — to slay this dragon and rescue Yeats? Perhaps. Another name for this dragon is Irish romanticism and it has swallowed many without a trace. In being a successful romantic Yeats has been a splendid painter and a bad influence. His example has provoked many failures. Instead of being a failure however (and cultivating its subtle pleasures) Yeats has triumphantly recognised that a central part of the Irish mythology is failure.

Failure is the Irish (and romantic) way of succeeding in in that it translates the glow of promise into the nostalgia of regret without anything in between. It substitutes rumour for achievement, word of mouth for the written word. Most Irish lives, as I remember them, were lived between promise and regret. Both have their darker shadow — a realism that rejects both, but at the price of a certain brutalism (visible in some Abbey Theatre kitchen comedy). This third party devotes much of its time to bitching about the promising and confirming the regretful. It reserves its most energetic attacks however for those who have betrayed both promise and regret by either achievement or genuine ambition. Such are the energies of the contemporary oral tradition.

Yeats's world is devoid of that brutalism and one misses it a bit. The dialectic of his art is promise and regret, both of which have virtuoso traditions. In Ireland the future was full of regret and the past was full of promise. Whatever its historical causes, this perversion in time — everyone was born old and grew younger (which explains late marriage) — seems inseparable from the Irish experience. At birth the weight of history was added to original sin, so growing old held the youthful promise of ditching both (Tir na nOg was a revealing invention). Consider the personifications of Ireland itself in a dazzling number of female mutations. She was old, she was young. She was a Queen and a Hag. She was promise and regret. She was mother and daughter and maintained with her sons and brothers a series of intimate relationships kept from incest only by the celebrated Irish continence. All those Gaelic poets had very chaste dreams of spéir-bheans. You could love Ireland but you couldn't bed her.

Promise and regret can be equated with two phrases — 'before it starts' and 'when it's over.' Almost all Yeats's paintings belong to these two formidable armies. On the one hand — youth, dawn, horses, encounters, gambling etc.; on the other — darkness, departures, evening, age, singing, commemorations, story-telling, reading. Common to both is the idea of *travelling*. No one has made a continuous list of Yeats's titles. They make up a litany — an idiosyncratic, poetic litany — of wayfarings and journeyings, which are traditionally haunted by 'to' and 'from', places of origin and destination. This is very romantic and Victorian. But what if there is no origin or destination — just travelling? Then the missing origin and destination become mythological inventions, and travel, deprived of its ends, is laden with symbolic meanings. Promise and regret are focussed by twin ideas — of the Quest and the Expulsion. It is the mythological power of these two conceits that helped sustain Yeats's lyric gift — as far as I know the most sustained lyric gift in the history of art (he was still achieving epiphanies of hope and regret when he was in his eighties).

78

The quest and the expulsion are deeply connected with Irish myth, and they were ways of escaping the impoliteness of the present — or of the chronological past experienced in the present. The present of course was always a casualty; in Ireland nothing is less real than the present. Every Irish child was trained in regret as Buddhist children are trained in meditation. Irish history (Carty's Irish History) telescoped centuries into one resentful block. Carrying it around was the Irish equivalent of ceremonial circumcision. One's past, like all the abbeys, all the castles, was in ruins, and any personal failure resonated comfortably through centuries. One was at least fulfilling one's destiny.

This chronological prison however was set between two timeless myths. There was, if you went back far enough, an ideal time, a golden age of gods and heroes. The authenticity of this was certified by the evidence reproduced in one's school-books — the Book of Kells and the Tara Brooch. An earlier state of grace was further certified by the shower of Celtic gold alighted in the National Museum. This nationalist Eden superimposed itself easily on the Biblical one. Eve (Ireland) sharing a platonic Eden with some monkish consort was betrayed by the English snake, and turned into a Poor Old Woman traipsing across centuries. Whenever there was any chance of freedom she grew vigorous and seductive to lead young men inflamed with patriotic passion into her service — identifying sexuality with death and of course redemptive grace ('he died for Ireland').

Ireland personified as a woman glimpsed here and there and perpetually in travel had a powerful imaginative resonance, since everyone who was anybody was also on the run — priests, poets, soldiers, heroes, teachers, all riskily slipping around and hiding and appearing and disappearing. You'd never know whom you might meet; the myth of the disguised eminence was thus vary practically sustained — right down to the 1920s when 'on-the-run' was a laden phrase baptising a Stranger and leading to hasty conspiratorial scuffles (it is not surprising that one of Yeats's most eminent celebrants — not critics — was Ernie O'Malley, a guerilla

79

fighter). If travelling was not a state of grace, it was close to it.

The other promise was of course freedom, a vision perpetually being deferred, until it also achieved a mythic status. The golden age of the past ('I walked entranced through a land of morn') was easily identified with the golden age of the future — that ultimate dawn deluded with innumerable false dawns (the title of one of Yeats's painting is 'The Last Dawn But One' — it was always the last dawn but one; note how this title stands between past and future, as between a pair of mirrors).

Freedom of course could also be experienced in travelling — a quasi kind of freedom but the only one available. It also to some degree reinstated the degraded present but giving it a certain timeless quality. (Irish patriots can be divided by their temporal coupling — for some like Pearse freedom was a very pure and abstract passion, for others of more practical, and in my view more heroic, vision, like Connolly, it was connected to economic and social realities. Generally speaking, Irish patriots were strong on nationalism and weak on ideology). The complicated apparatus that sustained the idea of freedom and promise was of course superfluous after freedom was attained—but the national character has a taste for the superfluous (as the Book of Kells demonstrates) — so the apparatus stayed around. Freedom was a great shock to the Irish. It was also a great shock to Jack Yeats's art, based as it was on the national vested interests of promise and regret.

This apparently instinctive connection with the two major forces that give the national myth its dialectical energy is what makes Jack Yeats a national painter. Thomas MacGreevy (that unfrocked courtier lost in his own dream of Ireland) was right in claiming that Yeats is to Ireland as, say, Watteau is to France. Yeats's access to the national imagination was quickened by late romanticism (everything except the Romanesque always happened late in Ireland; the Renaissance arrived in the eighteenth century). The patriot on the run is a romantic figure like those other outsiders approved in the

80

romantic canon — the madman, the criminal, the clown and acrobat . . . all paradigms for a soul the bourgeoisie felt they had lost. Hence Yeats's repertory (it is extraordinary how consistently expressionists — Yeats, Kokoschka, Ensor — establish their repertory companies of characters and themes) of tinkers, gypsies, sailors, circus performers, actors, travellers, tramps, jockeys, gamblers. This of course is only part of Ireland. The elliptical life involved in its strategies of encounter and avoidance has its uncelebrated and static twin. In mean little towns like Longford and Kinnegad and Mullingar promise and regret are drained by an immense boredom, a lassitude that reduces the blood to a treacle-like flow. Are there Emma Bovarys in such towns? One never sees this side of Ireland in Yeats's paintings, but it is just as much Ireland as the other.

If Yeats is a (or the?) national painter who colonises the regions of promise and regret through the themes of travelling, some questions follow. What was Yeats's attitude to Ireland? And what *persona* or mask did this involve?

II

By birth Yeats was an Anglo-Irishman (or Hiberno-Englishman?) and so separated from what he painted. But he wished to immerse himself in it ('the true painter must be part of the land and of the life he paints'). Therefore he mimicked his subjects, taking on some of their characteristics, prejudices, etc., and to some extent rejecting his own birthright — though the birthright of the Anglo-Irishman is not easy to define. This is a very complicated subject. First of all, I think there is little doubt that Yeats's ambition, however charmingly dissembled, was to be *the* national painter. He recognised his subject and pursued it with tenacity. No one has remarked on all the things Yeats didn't paint. He lived in England, visited the United States (courtesy of John Quinn) and was familiar with many parts of Europe, but he never, as far as I know, painted alien territory. He suppressed that fact that he had been born in

London, and indeed took an attitude to the English clearly informed by the prejudices of his constituency. His ambitions also reveal themselves in his mythological subjects, his contemporary sense (those paintings arising out of the revolution and civil war) and in the extraordinary attempt, in a series of late allegorical paintings, to generalise, like Kokoschka and Ensor (selections from the three artists would make a good exhibition), on major themes from his cast of characters.

There may have been some sibling rivalry in this to his brothers obvious and declared ambitions. Also his brother's magi-like utterances may have augmented that vernacular strain in Yeats's image of himself — as the good fellow who could *travel* (not drink or wench or fight) with the best of them. Yeats shared that desire with Synge and indeed in their travels through the West of Ireland together they make a luminous pairing. It is possible to mock this expedition (two genteel Anglo-Irishmen going native), but it is an authentic and repeated act of high culture (and if the Anglo-Irish represented anything, it was high culture) to restore itself through contact with a 'primitive' tradition — and thus, in a complicated series of reversals, add to that tradition.

The national painter belongs to a minority then. But the majority to which he was in the minority — the native Irish, defined themselves as a minority in relation to the English. Yet Yeats's direct relationship to the English was also as a member of a minority. He thus belonged to *three* minorities. (The pathos of the Anglo-Irishman's position has been insufficiently understood; as the big-house walls crumbled his barricades were reduced to culture, sport, an archaic accent, an air of superiority constantly drawn into a vacuum of unease. And he was always surrounded by the subversion of smiles. He didn't 'belong' anywhere either; unsustained by the mythologies of promise and regret he traversed the British Empire and its mythologies instead).

Yeats belonged to a majority only to the extent the native Irish identified him with the English. The traffic between these phantom minorities and majorities—with all possible permutations of misunderstanding, mimicking, dissembling, betrayal — make up the fabric of Irish society, more labyrinthine than any in Western Europe (with equivalents only in Eastern Europe and the Middle-East).

Yeats's task then was to exhibit to his country its own identity—which had been defined by its relationship to England, since England had donated the essential mythologies of promise and regret. The two countries are inextricably mixed in that each has mirrored the other through that rather magical displaced medium — the Anglo-Irishman. England's identity has been repeatedly reflected by Anglo-Irishmen from Congreve to Shaw; as Irishmen they brought what the English considered the vitality of the wild Irish into the drawing room by translating hostility into wit. Yet to the native Irish, the Anglo-Irishman brought what was considered English graces, an etiquette that could be dispensed with. This switch in direction gave Ireland a literature in English—and one painter.

In painting the Irish, Yeats was an outsider to the outsiders—and thus qualified for the task. (His colleagues in the Royal Hibernian Academy presented the Irish to themselves as picturesque primitives — entropic Rousseau). Yet there are pitfalls in this tinkering with and tapping of the national psyche, and any examination of Jack Yeats as national painter must take cognizance of them.

The Irishman's self-image as outsider was sold to him by a conqueror who purchased his nationality (i.e. manhood) in return for certain flatteries — the Irishman was witty, harddrinking, outrageous, poetic, capable of wild and impractical gestures, lovable, colourful in speech, picturesque in aspect (Jack Yeats characters?). He was also, in the twinkling of an eye, moody, cunning, untrustworthy, rebellious, incapable of responsibility. The dialogue between the two in the nineteenth century make up the fractured national character.

The critical moment in the exchange of stereotypes between conqueror and conquered (master and servant) occurs when the latter begins to confirm the image projected on him. At that moment, the rebel becomes the buffoon, who may rise to the high position of court jester. Charles Lever, whose father was English, represents in his early novels the moment when this transaction is taking place. Lever's sudden flights from and returns to England, his ambiguous attitude to his subject-matter, his carlessness in style, which is a kind of attempt to escape the subject-matter, can all be seen as embodying that moment when the stereotype is being formulated and accepted against his will, which is not even clear about what it is resisting. He is at the beginning of the tradition of the stage-Irishman, which Jack Yeats concludes. I am pointing out that this legend of the Irishman as romantic outsider is an English formulation. It is born of these lethal reciprocities we now understand better than we did — the bourgeois society exiles its subversive longing in the subject race which it then indulges between abrupt and savage repression. In this sense the romantic Irishman represents the Englishman's dream. (One has only to go to England to realise what a vested interest he has in preserving it).

Insofar as the Irish, deprived of their identity, concur with this image of themselves, they betray their own sense of nationality. Thus this stereotype — the Irishman as outsider — is the locus of great conflicts escaped only through constant travel. For in this freedom from responsibility inflicted by the master the servant sees the delusion of freedom, one augmented by mobility of whatever kind. Dignity is maintained by constantly changing the scenery. Changing the scenery is like changing one's face. The country is put on and off like a mask. The definition of freedom that the imagination is able to articulate in travelling is narrow, and fictional.

It is easy to see how travel is an escape from the stereotype (into some kind of freedom) and a confirmation of it (freedom from responsibility). So the only way the stereotype could be dignified was by making heroes of those of no fixed abode (still an address of honour in small Irish courts) — those vagrants in motion as much across the country's imaginative as well as physical landscape. Jack Yeats (and Synge — the two bear a comparison that has not been made)

84

faultlessly recognised that a certain dignity is to be purchased through travel, through its conjunction of glamour and loss (other names for promise and regret). But this apotheosis of travelling is sustained by all those dullards in the wings who stand for a degraded nation, and who eventually inherit those little citadels of boredom previously mentioned (and which in my opinion provides opportunities greater than the travelling man) — repetition, boredom, a very pure sense of time as a medium of non-progress. You don't find them in Jack Yeats—no shopkeepers, agents, gombeen men.

Yeats, an example of the great tradition of the Anglo-Irishman gone native, infuses the alien stereotype with national pride (which was just emerging). The way in which he did it is typical of the paradoxical transactions between master and servant. He suffused the stereotype with an excess of all its attributes, making the poetry more poetic, the rhetoric more rhetorical, the eccentric outlandish. Instead of parodying the parody and producing farce he made it, in an extraordinary exchange between a painter and a national image, heroic. In a transcendent gesture he flung back that image to the master—who is now revealed as cloddish, dull and venal (one projection returning another in the game of stereotypical tennis conducted between the two islands for nearly three centuries).

So the English were finally expelled by the fulfillment of an image they had imposed—the vagabond became the guerilla fighter, encounter became ambush and avoidance tactics. This tradition was carried into the Civil War; Jack Yeats of course took the outsider, Republican side against the new Free State. His brother, always well-disposed to the grandeur of institutions, became a Free State senator — one of many oppositions between the two. All these derive from their attitudes to the individual — W.B.'s great man emancipated himself from the people in proto-Fascist fashion; Jack Yeats's outsider is his exact opposite, the powerless traveller, alive with vernacular energies; and both men's *personae* exemplify this perfectly. Neither the dictator nor the rebel has much to do with the middle-classes, indeed the middle-classes confuse them. When the Republican outsider was finally absorbed into the political process, an enduring piece of Irish mythology was devitalized and altered.

The outsider was reduced to a small extremist organisation, and that shrinkage had much to do with the country's adoption of Yeats as national painter. For he provides access for a bourgeois society to a more or less fictional past. From inert little towns and farms came the men who ruled the country through the stagnant nineteen forties and fifties. For the new bourgeoisie (many of whom had been on the run themselves) the image of the outsider became their consolation and flattery. Part of the disillusion of the forties and fifties was that the bourgeoisie discovered that they weren't witty and poetic and marvellous at all. Nationhood proved that national image superfluous, and thus, in the rigorous law of Irish assimilation, it was made essential, but on a very different basis. The increasing distraction of Jack Yeats's are in the late forties and fifties shows this. His reaction to doubt was always further affirmation, even when the affirmation was forced into hectic postures.

III

Jack Yeats was lucky in handling that complicated vested interest — the myth of the national character. The conflict in this art is between the self-dramatization of a subject nation to accommodate a projected and humiliating image, and the narrow definitions of freedom the imagination was able to articulate in terms of travelling. His characters experienced this conflict on the level of style. The flick of a line becomes a commentary, and Yeats chatters away about his characters through nervously-inflected contours. His line — derived from an eighteenth century English tradition of caricature — is applied to heroic tasks which it occasionally caricatures with a redundant apocalypse. One is reminded of Synge's exploitation of the myth of Irish eloquence through a 'poetic' language that was never really spoken — though it seems just right to issue from the lips of Jack

Yeats's characters — and which occasionally lapses into parody. Synge's language has a built-in mirror—it is constantly reflecting itself. It is narcissus language, always regarding its own quirkiness, and is thus next door to condescension. That its natural users are not aware of its 'colourfulness', while we — in the audience — are, adds to the danger of this convention. Whatever their larger gestures, the line that defines them covers the figure with a veritable babble, especially in the later works. At the same time this commentary maintains the same convention as Synge's plays — that the subject is unaware of his own uniqueness. Such a vulnerable convention can only be justified by a powerful and consistent vision, which of course Yeats and Synge had.

This Dickensian connoisseurship of oddity is one of Yeats's potential weaknesses. He had an endless appetite for those annotations of character that make 'characters'. He accumulated the wayward with a collector's passion — whether it was in phrase or dress or gesture. Some characters in his novels are described by collections of observations, as if a character were the sum total of its eccentricities; then the character voyages into action flying all of them like pennants. (His subsequent actions however avoid a definition of his 'true' character; his eccentricities are brought into contact with those of other characters, and the slipping and gliding exchanges that result make up beautifully complicated and surprising *surfaces*. What saves the novels, I think, is the degree to which the language itself is identified with this stream of encounters — words and phrases rendezvous and salute each other with some of the outrageous aplomb and dignity which the characters maintain. Again, this attitude, like his line, is borrowed from the eighteenth century).

Yeats's caricaturing could of course go in two directions— towards the marvellous and towards the cliché. His extravagances lurch along, elegantly saving themselves from large falls and tumbles. The riskiness of his discourse in literature and painting give them spontaneity and excitement —even when one is surfeited one is convinced it is one's own

87

failure before Yeats's implacable optimism. However, Yeats's magnification of the observed detail is entirely consistent with the theme of travel; each transient is scrutinized for evidence of his recent history, as if his past actions protruded through his rags. The traveller bears himself from scrutiny to scrutiny; each new rest-station has this lidless eye. Yeats's magnified observation is a mode of access to a world where character is primary, the individual unique and actions are devoid of cant. In gaining access to this, Yeats faultlessly recognized one source he should draw on—the oral tradition—itself squeezed out between the forces of promise and regret. What the traveller says doesn't come out of a book, and Yeats repeatedly underlines his delight in the ballad—the traveller's story-book. His own atrocious verse (purposely so? A further hostility to his brother?) parodies the ballad form with schoolboy delight.

One of Yeats's concerns was very much connected to the theme of travelling. He was mad about adventure stories — *boy's* adventure stories. It is usual to look on Yeats's early tales and toy theatres and illustrations with a sentimental indulgence I cannot summon. (One important result of this theatrical concern is the stage-set aspect of his painting, which continued to the end. His paintings use all the devices of the proscenium stage. So does most narrative painting, but Yeats used them *theatrically* — emphasizing the picture space as a theatre of illusions). More important than the value of this early work (which I think is slight) is the way Yeats brought the moral healthiness of the boy's adventure story to his mature art, and would allow nothing to disturb it. Promise is the mainspring of the adventure story and to the end of his life Yeats rejected anything that would discharge that promise. This persistence of boyhood (and his father's great portrait of Jack Yeats as a boy in the Dublin National Gallery uncannily foresees this) was a protection from complicated moral issues that would have qualified his vision. Childhood experience carries its own certificate of authenticity. By refusing to grow up, Yeats preserved his capacity to transform experience into myth and myth into

88

experience. He also avoided responsibility through innocence and the theme of travel. While this strategy—however unconscious—was necessary to Yeats's vision, it excluded from his universe certain areas of experience and moral judgment. (The exacerbated moral conscience inseparable from expressionism is absent here. Yeats's innocence has been attractive especially to those without it — Kokoschka and Beckett come to mind.)

This is much more obvious in the novels than in the paintings where it arises in only one area and there turns out to be an advantage. Yeats never painted a nude—there are no nudes in adventure stories. This puritanism is entirely in keeping with his status as national painter — as a force giving an idealistic chastity to his visions. This modesty is extended to all his themes, no matter how apocalyptic. There is a pressure *against* disclosure, a quality that gives his characters a breeding their flamboyance would seem to exclude. This delicacy is seen particularly in pictures of single characters alone; one almost hears the audience's respectful hush in order not to violate the privacy of the character onstage. All Yeats's 'under the rose' symbolism is a form of this modesy. Travelling is also 'under the rose' and between the traveller and the host there is a tension involving an ethics of disclosure—so that curiosity meanders around the traveller, which he titillates without destroying by unnecessary revelation. Thus the iconography of travel — clothes, accents, gestures, phrases — is amplified and read with great virtuosity in kitchens all over Ireland. Indeed the traveller always remains mysterious, while his gestures are remembered.

In this the traveller is very like Irish history, which also tends to be remembered not as a chronological sequence, but as a series of gestures — speeches from the dock, farewells and flights, brief visions and betrayals, hunger strikes, pinings and executions, acts of individual daring in a theatre of futility. As gestures, these describe the surface of things which remain mysterious and they are inseparable from promise and regret. Though the gesture explains neither, it enables them to be re-experienced in proper mythic fashion. The gesture, the language of the dispossessed, resonates in the national psyche.

Yeats's sensitivity to gesture is visible in all his work, and is seen par excellence in his play 'In Sand'. The writing of a simple memorial on the sand is passed from one generation to another, survives its meaning, and becomes mysterious on (literally) a foreign shore. Myth is proved superior to history. Writing on sand becomes more durable than on marble, testifying, as Jack Yeats's work always does, to the survival of the intimate over the 'important' things. This concern with gesture is the key to Jack Yeats's universe, and to the country whose mythologies he so powerfully re-enacts.

All Yeats's character gesture. The paint that describes them also gestures. In this his work recalls Magnasco whose livid strokes set phantoms gesturing in an unearthly nature. Yeats's paint never ceases to travel in ribbons and cycles, always avoiding repose with faultless rhythms. There is a continual dialogue between predictability and surprise. Yeats, in one of his few comments about painting, said 'An artist should avoid convention, even when the convention is his own invention'. This re-enacts in paint the strategies of encounter and avoidance in which his figures partake. Colour planes are never elaborated. Instead Yeats *draws* with colour — often colour outlines a line in an inside-out technique that gives a radiance to his figures. The gestures of the figures, involved in the mythology of travelling, and the gestures of the paint, itself travelling ceaselessly, begin to amplify each other. The paint itself begins to become a mythic medium.

To this is added another series of changes. When travelling the dawn, darkness and the weather are big events. The weather in Yeats' paintings reflect not those sodden days when the earth is audibly soaking, but those mutable days when translucent skies scatter the light through veils of rain, and colour starts up everywhere. The weather itself augments the sense of change and movement. Even the furniture of his pictures is often temporary — make-shift shelters and carnival flats that look as if they could be removed, circus fashion, to the next picture.

With a shock one recognises that Yeats has successfully identified his medium with his figures, his scenery, his theme, his country and its mythology of travel. The medium is Ireland and Ireland is the medium. This gives to his work authority and to his paint that extraordinary sense of medium which is his main painterly contribution. Is is hardly a formal contribution. But for a painter to successfully identify a country's mythology with his medium is, to my knowledge, unique. To accomplish this required a country with a dominant myth, shared imaginatively by its people. Yeats placed the medium not just at the service of his own imagination but of a collective identity which was sentenced by history to travel for centuries between the futile harbours of promise and regret.

MIXED METAPHORS;
JACK B. YEATS'S WRITINGS

by Marilyn Gaddis Rose

On January 4, 1941, Jack B. Yeats sent some friends a New Year's greeting to their race horse: '. . . I wish that Cottage Rake may always find himself with the cream of the social sailing, like a bird over all obstacles, including mixed metaphors . . . .'[1] This whimsical expression, typical apparently of Yeats's conversation and casual writing, is demonstratably typical of his published writing. His plays and novels are mixed metaphors in every sense. They depend on incongruities and far-fetched juxtapositions; the caprices of personality and providence, which make up their plots, are at best bittersweet; and they themselves as works of literature are generic hybrids. Each of our assertions would describe as well his paintings which are continually surprising, poignantly narrative, and technically original. However, when he makes his material visible with paint, he is far more satisfying than when he makes it legible with words. We do not mean that he is a genius as a painter but merely talented as a writer. Rather, we mean that when he paints he transforms his material and turns it into an object complete in itself, but when he writes he merely rearranges it and leaves it with evident lacunae of meaning and form. Is this because in both substance and structure he has less control over his material when he writes? Or is this a function of the medium being used? Both conjectures are probably correct. In any event, his stories, dramatised or fictionalised, are mixed products. That is their shortcoming; that is their strength.

It is tempting to surmise that his fantasies and fears,

---

1 To Mr. and Mrs. F. C. Vickerman, Dublin, who kindly granted permission to quote.

transfigured if not exorcised when translated into lines, forms, and colours, remain haunting and fearsome when only verbalised, as if words did not sufficiently distance him from them. It may well be also that as viewers of a painting we tolerate a greater degree of Kantian purposiveness without purpose than we do as readers of a novel or spectators of a play. And it is a fact in the history of each art that the public must become acclimatised to new modes of expression. Thus Yeats's painting, especially that of his final period, 1927-1955, could profit from at least seventy-five years of training of public taste, whereas his writing, an anticipation of the Theatre of the Absurd and the New Novel, would have to wait twenty-five years for a hospitable public.

The metaphors of his paintings, essentially narrative usually having literary titles,[2] are strong because of vigorous line, geometric blocking, and sure colouring; profound because of complex texture and subtle line diffusion. It would be extravagant to claim that he transfers analogous procedures of line, blocking, and colour to his writing. He does adhere to a basic plot: life lived adventurously defines man's adaptability. He does carry over to writing texture and diffusion, but with a different medium, of course, he gains a different effect. The result is that his paintings bewitch us, and his writings dumbfound us.

In short, the qualities which in his painting lead from complexity to beauty and, hence, to pleasureable satisfaction in the viewer, in his writing lead from complexity to confusion and, hence, to amused exasperation in the reader and spectator. With paint Yeats achieves harmony and completeness; with words, disharmony and incompleteness. In his writing we receive from plot progression, dialogue, and imagery an impression of authorial helplessness. The plots are alternately meandering and precipitous; the dialogue is

---

2 A thesis persuasively demonstrated by Professor Martha Caldwell in an unpublished paper 'Sources of the Art of Jack B. Yeats', delivered to the meeting of the American Committee for Irish Studies, May 11, 1968, Cortland, New York.

random, advancing the ostensible plot only to take it in an unforeseen direction; the imagery as situation, scene, and prop follows only the logic of free association. With such Sternesque structure, gratuitousness is nearly inevitable — only the unpredictable will happen. Comic trappings are ineffectual, especially since tragedy always lurks and usually occurs. With hapless men at the mercy of a prankster god who created them in his image, contempt for mankind looms nearly as large as charity, for what is man if not a perpetrator and butt of jokes? Yet these characteristics, which could be solely shortcomings, recommend his writings to us all the more and keep him from being a mere curiosity in Anglo-Irish regionalism. Paradoxical as it may seem, Yeats undoubtedly without premeditation, is probably more original and profound in his writing than in his painting. In devising mixed experiences for us, he was a quarter century ahead of his time.

Yeats, like, say, Kokoschka and Henri Michaux, affords a case study for the relationship between literature and painting. Like the Austrian Expressionist, incidentally, an admiring acquaintance, and the Belgian Surrealist, his works in both media are mutually analogous, so much so that the description of one will fit the other. There is a surprisingly close correlation chronologically and stylistically between what Yeats wrote and what he drew.

By and large, his first period of painting, roughly 1888 to 1919, correlates with the plays which he wrote for the miniature stage. During this time, he used chiefly water colour and India ink in bold lines. His drawings of this period, for example, 'Whirly Horses in the Rain' (1891) or 'The Tinker' (1895) use soft hues firmly outlined and cross-hatched in the manner of an academy trained cartoonist like Briggs, the American master whom John B. Yeats commended to his son, or of a good poster artist like Toulouse-Lautrec and his imitators. These drawings are of a piece with the sets and illustrations of these plays, which likewise are deliberately crude in execution and substance. These plays include *James Flaunty or the Terror of the Western Sea* (1901), *The*

Treasure of the Garden (1902), *The Scourge of the Gulph* (1903), and *A Little Fleet* (1904). He published no major work during his second period, 1919 to 1927, when he used oil on flat unemphatic surfaces, carrying over some water colour techniques into oil painting. Perhaps his desire to tell a story was fulfilled by his painting during these years, for this was when he produced such unambiguous canvasses as 'Bachelor's Walk' and 'The Funeral of Harry Boland' (both 1922), which are as remarkable for their subdued patriotism as for their subdued colour and subtle pyramid disposition. The move into his final and best known period of Expression-istic painting, 1927 to 1955, when he ceased to paint, was gradual, but once established contrasted with the preceding periods and stayed consistent with itself. Here is where we find the knowingly dissipated line and the complex textured application of paint and innovative use of colour. The pub-lication of his mature works of writing begins at this time also. Once this late style of writing is established, it does not change in manner or implication. The novels are: *Sligo*, 1930; *Sailing Sailing Swiftly*, 1933; *The Amaranthers*, 1936; *The Charmed Life*, 1938; *Ah Well, A Romance in Perpetuity*, 1942; *And to You Also*, 1944; *The Careless Flower*, 1947. The plays are the three plays in *Apparitions*, 1933; *Harlequin's Positions*, performed in 1939 but still unpublished; *La La Noo*, performed in 1942, published 1960; and *In Sand*, performed in 1949 and published with *The Green Wave* in 1964.[3]

In terms of sophistication and development, these latter are at the far end of the spectrum from the plays for the miniature stage. But the themes remain the same. From jaunty James Flaunty, barely saved from execution, to the pompous Governor of *In Sand*, barely saved from suicide, each work exploits the same fears, and fails to neutralise them with the same tenuous compensations offered by life. The pain of separation, exile, old age, death, family strife,

---

3 Miss Anne B. Yeats graciously lent me copies of the plays for the miniature stage and a typescript of 'Harlequin's Positions'.

and betrayal in friendship can be only temporarily alleviated by the pleasure of love, parenthood, friendship, reverie, and escape. For each source of pleasure contains also the source of pain. The beloved spouse can die; the cherished child can grow up and go away; the never-never land of escape can become a maze of dangers and frustrations. The creatures who survive these ill-bred cosmic jokes can thank their own caution, sense of humour, and good luck.[4]

If after a brief review of these works we look particularly at three representative works which use kindred plots and props, the miniature stage play *The Scourge of the Gulph,* the novel *The Amaranthers,* and the play *In Sand,* we shall see these three illustrated; first, the continuity within Yeats's writing; second, its relationship to his painting as a presentation of compulsions which pictorial representation can assuage; and third, its use, before the fact, of the conventions of the New Novel and the Absurd play.

All the plays for the miniature stage are horrendous tales of *Peter Pan* type swashbuckling. *Sligo* is a stream-of-conscious fictionalised reminiscence. *Sailing Sailing Swiftly* follows three generations of an Anglo-Irish family whose happiness, while real, is continually upset by freak accidents. *The Charmed Life,* a one-sided dialogue, follows the peregrinations of the narrator Mr. No Matter and his companion Bowsie to a resort hotel for a dance closing the summer season. Before festivities begin, one guest dies from over-exposure, Bowsie plummets backwards into a gully and is presumed dead, and the corpse of a young man drowned earlier is washed ashore. *Ah Well, A Romance in Perpetuity* sounds like Sligo also. It is a reminiscence treating death and resurrection in a ludicrous manner with an episode like that of Synge's *In the Shadow of the Glen. And to You Also* is a first-person monologue haunted by death sequences. *The*

---

4 See my discussion 'Sub Rosa: The Writings of Jack B. Yeats'. *Eire-Ireland,* III (Summer, 1968), 37-47; 'Solitary Companions in Beckett and Jack B. Yeats', *Eire-Ireland,* IV (Summer, 1969), 66-80.

Careless Flower begins in a carefree manner with a Sunny Isles cruise but incorporates shipwreck, backruptcy, natural death, revolution, and accidental death before it is over. Revolution and accidental death in a never-never land also fell the luckless heir in the play *Rattle* in *Apparitions,* for the 'rattle' is a death rattle. Death awaits the befriending hero in *The Old Sea Road* in the same collection, when he accepts a poisoned drink from the man whom he is trying to help. And the citizens of Pullickborough, who try to discourage the apparition of the title play, have their hair first turn white from fear and then dyed with red ink by the barber who for some undisclosed reason has always hated them. *La La Noo* avoids unmotivated human evil but shows human bungling and apathetic good will bringing about death also. The only thinking character, the Stranger, who is going to drive some stranded women to a bus stop, breaks his neck against a tree while backing out a lorry. *The Green Wave,* a conversation piece in one act, substitutes misunderstanding and resignation for tragedy and bitterness. 'The Green Wave' is a painting, perhaps similar to Monet's 'Impression. Soleil levant', which the First Elderly Man owns and loves and which his friend the Second Elderly Man makes no effort to appreciate. The former adapts to the situation by offering his friend a drink. All of the works illustrate that try as he can, the only place man can go is nowhere and the best he can do is not to die on the way.

Let us look at this predicament in more detail. *The Scourge of the Gulph* in its four brief scenes (a scant thirteen pages of text) displays a fearful and futile sequence of events resulting from a misguided and exaggerated sense of honour (like the *pundonor* plots in Spanish literature).[5] In scene i, Captain Carricknagat for an insult to his wife has just had

---

5 All quotations are from the following editions: *The Scourge of the Gulph* (London: Elkin Mathews, 1903); *The Amaranthers* (London: Heinemann, 1936); *In Sand* (Dublin: Dolmen Press, 1964). Miss Anne B. Yeats and Mr. Michael B. Yeats have kindly given me permission to quote from these works.

97

Joseph Miles flogged. In scene ii, the Captain receives the letter which his wife, captured by savages during a search for water, wrote before dying. He reads her request that he retrieve her skull from the middle tree. In scene iii, the Captain and the Bosun, sole survivors, sight the middle tree. In scene iv, the Captain, bearing the skull in a chest, is shot by Miles, who exclaims, 'An empty skull, a black box, a dead skipper! Have I done anything or nothing?' In this compressed saga of violence, we find sea-faring Anglo-Irish, deprived of their moral bearings by a critical situation in a tropical locale, responding by inappropriate reflexes. Survival in a new situation calls for a new code emphasizing forgiveness and cooperation, but these characters, the hardiest of the crew presumably, can carry out only rituals relevant in their old society: flogging for alleged disrespect to a female, sentimental quest for mortal remains, murder for revenge and greed. Miles's moment of lucidity, his grasp of the existential absurd, to use Camus's terms, comes too late to help anyone, himself included. Stranded as he is on a paradise turned hell, he will soon discover that his acts have been more than unprofitable and cruel; they will be self-destructive as well. Although the characters are intentionally caricatures with as few aspects of third-dimensional fleshiness as the sharply outlined cartoon-like illustrations, they are related to the more developed and subtle characterizations which we shall find in Yeats's later work. They are puzzling and incomplete because we know so little of their background and have so short a space to watch them in action. We are not puzzled by the flat perspectives of water colours of the same period, for example, 'The Tinker' referred to earlier or 'The Music' (1898) or 'Mother' (1903). We can speculate about the fortunes of the three street musicians in 'The Music' or about the clown and the fat lady in 'Mother', but it is not incumbent upon us to do so, for their pictorial reality is ordered and complete Yet the lapses of situation and character-logic in the playlet, puzzling as they are, are merely exaggerations of the ill-logic in life and are tendencies to be developed by the Theatre of the Absurd. For example,

98

the characters cannot really speak to one another; there is a marked discrepancy between causes and effects that can be explained only by the essential gratuitousness of man in the universe. Although this playlet is a product of the Belle Epoque, it gives a very contemporary assessment of death and solitude — illustrated by the sole character Miles and his macabre possessions — as the only sure ends.

In *The Amaranthers* life is a practical joke which works to the partial advantage of the characters who stay in a state of willed hilarity. They are like the three figures in 'Shouting' (1950) who may be carousing with glee or shrieking for help, since we cannot tell whether the open-eyed character in the shelter at right rear-ground is staring from glassy inebriation or untended death. Yeats gives no clues in the novel either; he warns us at the outset that we shall not be able to make anything out of his inconsequential free associations: 'But the Ole Man River automobile endlessness, watches by the ring-side with an endless chain of eyes, and that not a symbol, for there is none' (p. 5). The name 'amaranthers' from the flower which never fades but is sometimes called 'love-lies-bleeding' indicates a cycle of pleasure and pain.

In Part I the Amaranthers are a club of eternal adolescents whose rooms are raided by police on the unfounded charge of Communism. The place may well be Dublin, although some characters seem too much like professional Irishmen to be real ones. The survivors and their janitor recoup their fortunes on an Island where they convert a six-storey building into another clubhouse. The author wanders off into an amusing account of a performance of *Old Care* given by some local culture-mongers (a section that makes us suspect some in-group Sligo joke). Part II picks up without apparent reference to Part I. Proceeding in a much more random fashion, it deals with a Dublin peddler James who averts a pony-car accident in England, marries the pony-owner's sister, and on the death of brother and sister goes off to South America, apparently, to live on their railroad dividends. When the dividends stop, he takes a steamer to someplace more primitive, disembarks prematurely and has many adventures with a guide named OhOh before reaching a government outpost. Proceeding thence to the capital of whatever country it is, he trades his railroad script for the private Pullman car of the railroad president and takes off on a never-never track which runs to Hollywood. There he he rounds up movie hopefuls for the Great Man of moviedom. But it is a never-never Hollywood, also, and when a hurricane comes up, he and his entourage go back to rescue the unidentified Irish Island of Part I. When last seen, he is taking the Amaranthers to live forever in his Pullman car. The circumstances are, as Yeats's remark warned us earlier, endless. The plot is constantly on the move, and just as constantly derailing. It is never over and, hence, never complete. On the next to the last page is a paradigmatic statement of Yeats's process of composition and free-wheeling circularity: 'And first you begin to stop emptying your heads, every time they begin to fill with thoughts, and then you will begin to think, and then you will stop thinking and begin to talk . . . And then you will stop talking and begin to fancy, and then you will stop fancying and begin to imagine. And by that time it will be morning. Some morning' (p. 272).

Here we have the macabre props of *The Scourge of the Gulph* obscured by a plethora of weird accoutrements and death and disaster obscured by a multitude of swashbuckling adventures. Obscured but not neutralized, for the accoutrements and adventures are so eccentric that we tend to discount them. The same formula of action is discernible: the characters are tried by experience, humorously, to be sure, in their home milieu, an English milieu, and various exotic milieux. Their collective response throughout is that of a prankster more light-hearted than lucid and resourceful, who counts on good luck to get him through. Good luck does, but, inasmuch as the plot is an endless chain of fortuities, it might just as well have not. Digression nearly replaces progression here. The plot moves so unaccountably that it seems to go in every direction at once. In the final analysis, characters are as one-dimensional as in the plays for the miniature stage. Only the implied narrator is felt as a presence.

Props are dropped too quickly to become anything more than a subliminal image, and if we avoid being exasperated, we are teased. These remarks could be made about the New Novel as well. Robbe-Grillet, Sarraute, and Pinget, or Yeats's compatriots Beckett and Flann O'Brien often weary us with their elusive narrators, Freudianly slippery props and lay themselves open to the charge of inexcusable verbosity. Robbe-Grillet, Sarraute, Pinget, and Beckett may be as capable of inventiveness as Yeats and O'Brien, but unlike the latter, they prefer to use monotony as a device and make us negate events A, B, and C by continually revising them. Yeats does not erase anecdotes by revision. Here as in all his novels, he makes us negate event A by the contradictory preposterousness of B and C. For example, if James were in Central or South America in the late 1930s, he could not have taken a Pullman car to Hollywood, and if he were in Hollywood, he could not have got to the Ireland-like Island, and from no point from thence would a Pullman car have been very useful. Yet his apparent acceptance of fictional reality makes him no less pessimistic than these cosmopolitan authors of studied bleakness, for his stopping point is not a happy ending but a happy accident.

Once again, we notice that the medium chosen makes *The Amaranthers* predictably like and unlike the paintings of his final period. Take for example, 'He Seeks His Fortune' (1947). Here the whitened figure of the left centre foreground, although brushed in with rough strokes, conveys a conviction of bravery. He is a man who fearlessly strides away from the teal blue and gold shore into the dark unknown (cf. Frost's 'Come In' [1942], ll. 15-16: 'Almost like a call to come in/To the dark and lament'). The roughness may seem casual, but the direction of the strokes and the hues force our eyes away from, but always back to, the man who deserves our admiration. The diffuseness and randomness found in *The Amaranthers* could be ascribed to this canvas; moreover, this man, moving away from the seacoast — as the characters in the novel do repeatedly — is likewise overwhelmed by the proportions of the setting.

Brave as he may be, only good luck will get him through. Yet his purpose fills the canvas. The metaphor of the title is represented completely and to our satisfaction. It is his seeking that imposes, not the problematic goal of his search. But the medium of language and the expectations of the traditional novel, which a New Novel exploits, make us want an explanation of the Amaranthers' restlessness, James's wanderlust and how the two fit together. The painting could be only what it is, but the novel could have every episode replaced, so gratuitous does each one seem.

In Sand, like *The Scourge of the Gulp* and *The Amaranthers*, takes us from Ireland to a fabulous site where delight is expected and danger lurks. Act I, a Dublin autumn many years ago, begins with a scene like the painting 'The Sick Bed' (1950), where a haler, younger friend cheers an invalid. Tony Larcson, on his deathbed, asks that a nice little girl be chosen to go with due pomp to the far Strand and write with a stick in the sand, 'TONY, WE HAVE THE GOOD THOUGHT FOR YOU STILL' (p. 19). He asks that a trust fund be held for her until she is twenty-one. A few weeks later a little girl named Alice carries out his wish.

In Act II, twelve years later, Alice, who has spent her legacy on a seashore holiday, is found writing the phrase by Maurice, an older man, who proposes to her and in turn writes the phrase again. They are followed by the maid who writes the phrase for the chauffeur. Ten years later, Alice and Maurice, completing a world cruise somewhere in Oceania, are writing the memorial in the sand when notified of their bankruptcy.

The setting has abruptly changed from a South Seas idyll to the inadequately masked unhappiness of the canvas 'South Pacific' (1937), where in a lush tropical setting a clownesque colonial and a servant in black face cannot avoid postures of despair.

Many years later, Act III, Alice sells sea-shells for a living. An Old Sailor, merely an ominous allusion in Act II, tells a Tourist of the vagaries of his Island existence. It was he who had taught Maurice the song 'Captain Death's got his hand on my shoulder' (p. 37). Now the Old Sailor explains, 'He is a noble Captain, he isn't of this world nor yet of the next. He's a kind of go-between . . .' (p. 53). He concludes, 'The only thing I'm sure of is that I will die and I knew that from the first' (p. 54). Scenes ii, iii, and iv follow rapidly a year later. Alice and the Old Sailor have died, and it appears that the Tourist and the Governor will attempt a coup d'état. The Governor recalls that before dying, Alice was seen writing in the sand: 'After the lady had left the strand I sent one of my attendants down to see for himself what was written. But the tide had risen over it, whatever it was' (p. 57). A sudden influx of pre-season tourists cancels the coup d'état. As the dejected Governor sits down in the moonlight, two native lovers appear. The boy asks the girl to write in the sand for luck. The Brown Girl says, 'I'll write what we have always written . . .TONY-WE-HAVE-THE-GOOD-THOUGHT-FOR-YOU-STILL'. The Governor, still dejected, copies the phrase and tries to shoot himself. But the lovers prevent his suicide, and the Brown Girl comforts him with the curtain line, 'The tide is coming in now fast, look, look, the waters are covering up and washing away everything that we have written' (p. 79).

Violence has been averted, but death has been only postponed. The Governor and the Tourist have as much difficulty in adapting to a disorienting situation as do Captain Carricknagat and Joseph Miles in *The Scourge of the Gulph*. The characters in this play are as dependent upon the whims of providence as is James in *The Amaranthers*. Yeats's outlook is more mellow, and, correspondingly, the outcome of the play is more mixed. Alice and the Old Sailor do respond rationally rather than automatically to a new situation. Yet we can hardly envy them, for they are in want. Tony Larcson's deathbed wish is still being carried out — but a half a world away by people who never knew him and could not have understood him. Ritual has changed the message from the remembrance of a particular human being to a talisman for any man. And the words which man writes get just as regularly washed away. The play which began very regionally has ended with a larger-than-life metaphor on life where human achievements are like words traced in the sand.

Like a serious play of the Theatre of the Absurd *In Sand* makes a metaphysical statement as the culmination of a dialectical series of happenings. Of course, plays by Shaw, Pirandello, and O'Neill do this also without being for all that pre-Absurd. However, these masters, for all the theatricality which they may exploit, O'Neill particularly, rely on a situation which seems initially plausible and which involves an action with a recognizable beginning, middle, and end. Their characters are sufficiently individualized to seem like real people. *In Sand*, like Brecht in Epic Theatre or like Beckett and Ionesco of the Theatre of the Absurd, starts with a contrived situation. If it weren't for Alice who grows up, grows old, and dies, the episodes would be nearly interchangeable. Like Brecht's or Beckett's and Ionesco's plays, *In Sand* divides arguments among stereotypes who are vague (Tony, Alice), grotesque (Governor, Tourist), or archetypal (Old Sailor, Brown Girl). The dialogue, adumbrating a debate, rather than advancing a plot, imposes a slow psychological pace. (The play could be directed to play at a fair degree of speed, as can be done with *The Rhinoceros* or *The Chairs*.) By reiteration of motif — here the greeting to Tony — and by slowing down action and making very little stage business necessary, the dialogue encourages us to internalize the play in terms of images rather than actions, as we tend to do also when watching Absurd plays like Beckett's *Endgame*, Ionesco's *The Lesson*, or Pinter's *The Dumb Waiter*.

Although the curtain line is a pronouncement, *In Sand*, no more than the plays just mentioned, resolves the issues which it raises. It is thus analogous to paintings of the same period, for example, 'The Basin in which Pilate washed his hands' (1951) and 'Discovery' (1953), but, inevitably, less realized. These paintings represent situations of uncertainty with techniques which underscore the subject. Both have lines which materialize as recognizable objects only if we study them and let our vision adapt to their implicit forms.

The former canvas, based on Lady Gregory's *The Tidings Brought by Bridget*, shows an open air performance at a country fair. Against a central vertically stroked pyramid of purple and rose a face beseeches a throned figure. We have in focus before us the inability to hear and the inability to be heard, in short, the failure of communication, a persistent theme in the Theatre of the Absurd. The latter canvas shows a man with Yeats's own strong-jawed face walking resolutely into a tunnel of trees, away from a clearing which is the only way out of the darkness which he has entered; the brush strokes force our eyes back to his gaze. The painting allegorizes as a journey to death or a quest to the unknown; the expression of the face is glazed as if the man were making a discovery which took all his courage. In the first painting we do not know what the king hears; in the second, we do not know what the man sees, but the medium allows us to contemplate the act rather than its object. *In Sand*, like plays of the Theatre of the Absurd, is prevented by its own conventions from being overly explicit. But our expectations, built by familiarity with traditional plays, including those of Shaw, Pirandello, and O'Neill, who revitalized tradition, make us look for goals and final causes beyond the text.

Yeats probably did not foresee that fiction and drama would catch up with him. (He died six days before the première of *Endgame* in Paris.) Indeed, he tended to deprecate his own writing. Shortly before his death when he learned that the British Broadcasting Company Third Programme would revive *In Sand*, he remarked to his dealer Victor Waddington, 'They're trotting this out . . . I wish they'd forget this stuff . . . They should remember me as a painter.'[6]

He is unfair to himself. We should remember him as painter and poet. His writing has a value that extends beyond the whimsical charms and veiled threats of its mixed metaphors.

6 Personal conversation, August 31, 1966, the Clarendon House, London.

From the standpoint of literary history, his writing was predictive. It shows how much we used to count on plots going from here to there, characters whom we could have met, images that belong to the common stock of Western symbols. It shows how much we gain when we readers and spectators must collaborate with the author. Now that the Theatre of the Absurd and the New Novel have trained our taste, his works seem very modern to us and no longer erratic. We are accustomed to self-negating plots, characters freed from customary motivations, and elusive symbols.

From the standpoint of the arts, his writing adumbrates the on-going definitions of the distinctions between literature and painting. As a case study, Yeats suggests that fantasizing in words does not quite effect a safe distance from the fearful and phantasmal. In painting, colour and line put the inspiration where it can only be contemplated, where it can only be embellished, where it can be fixed, complete at a point of becoming. Verbal pictures are not equivalent. We are closer to the material, and we cannot neutralize it by disguising it or satirizing it. If we push it away, it can still return. If we write it down, the tide will still wash it away.

He uses the same metaphors for his writings as for his paintings. If the latter are pure, the former are mixed. Verbal sketches of pictures which he often drew, they are partial paintings.

JACK B. YEATS

A CHRONOLOGY OF MAJOR PERSONAL EVENTS, PUBLICATIONS AND EXHIBITIONS.

by Martha Caldwell

1871:   Born 29 August at 23 Fitzroy Street, London.

1879-87:   Lived with grandparents in Sligo.

1887:   Joined family at 58 Eardley Crescent, Earl's Court, London.

1888:   3 Blenheim Road, Bedford Park became the residence of the Yeats family. Jack B. Yeats attended several art classes including those at the Westminster School of Art under Frederick Brown.

1892:   Worked for a short time in Manchester for the David Allen Poster Firm.

1894:   Married Mary Cottenham White on August 23rd at Emmanuel Church, Gunnersbury. They lived at The Chestnuts, Eastworth, Chertsey, Surrey.

1898:   Jack B. Yeats and his wife moved to Snail's Castle (Cashlauna Shelmiddy) at Strete, near Dartmouth in Devon. They made a trip to Venice and northern Italy.

1900:   Death of mother, Susan Pollexfen Yeats.

1901:   Publication of *James Flaunty*.

1902:   Publication of *A Broadsheet*.

1903:   Publication of *A Broadsheet, The Scourge of the Gulph*, and *The Treasure of the Garden*.

1904:   Jack Yeats and his wife spent a few months in New York. Publication of *The Bosun and the Bob-Tailed Comet*.

1905:   June and July was spent travelling with John M. Synge, illustrating Synge's articles on the congested districts of Ireland for *The Manchester Guardian*.

1908:   *A Broadside* published by the Cuala Press. John Butler Yeats went to New York and remained there until his death in 1922.

1909:   *A Broadside* published and *A Little Fleet*.

1910:   *A Broadside* published. The Yeatses moved in the late summer to Red Ford House, Greystones, Co. Wicklow. Yeats began to paint consistently in oils.

1911:   Publication of *A Broadside* and *Synge and the Ireland of his Time* by W. B. Yeats with a Note of Walk through Connemara with him by Jack B. Yeats. Publication of *Jack B. Yeats: His Pictorial and Dramatic Art* by Ernest Marriott.

1912:   Publication of *A Broadside* and *Life in the West of Ireland*.

1913:   *A Broadside* published.

1914:   *A Broadside* published.

1915:   *A Broadside* published. On July 19th Jack Yeats was elected an Associate Member of the Royal Hibernian Academy.

1916:   On July 20th Jack Yeats was elected a member of the Royal Hibernian Academy.

1917:   The Yeatses moved to 61 Marlborough Road, Donnybrook, Dublin.

1922:   John Butler Yeats died in New York on February 2nd. Publication of *Modern Aspects of Irish Art*.

1923:   W. B. Yeats was awarded the Nobel Prize in Poetry on November 16th.

1929:   In the fall the Yeatses moved to 18 Fitzwilliam Square in Dublin.

1930:   Publication of *Sligo*.

1933:   Publication of *Sailing Sailing Swiftly* and *Apparitions*.

1936:   Publication of *The Amaranthers*.

1938:   Publication of *The Charmed Life*.

1939:   W. B. Yeats died on January 28th. *Harlequin's Position* produced at the Abbey Experimental Theatre, June 5-17.

1940:   Jack B. Yeats joined the Victor Waddington Galleries in Dublin. On January 16th Lollie died. 'British Painting Since Whistler' Exhibition at the National Gallery, London.

1942:   Nicholson and Yeats' Exhibition at the National Gallery, London. Publication of *Ah Well, A Romance in Perpetuity*. *La La NOO* produced at the Abbey Theatre on May 3rd.

1943:   *La La NOO* published.

1944:   Publication of *And To You Also*.

1945:   National Loan Exhibition in Dublin at National College of Art. *Jack B. Yeats* by Dr. Thomas MacGreevy published.

108

1946: In February Jack Yeats was awarded an honorary degree by Trinity College, Dublin.

1947: Mary Cottenham White Yeats (Cottie) died on April 28th. *The Careless Flower* published. On July 8th Jack Yeats was awarded on honorary degree (D.Litt.) by the National University of Ireland.

1948: Exhibition of Jack Yeats's paintings at the Tate Gallery, London and elsewhere, organised by the Arts Council of Great Britain.

1949: Lily Yeats died on January 5th. *In Sand* produced at the Abbey on April 19th. Jack Yeats was awarded honorary membership in the Adriatica Cultural Academy, Milan.

1950: On February 13th Jack B. Yeats was invested Officer of the Legion of Honor.

1951-52: Retrospective Exhibition of Jack Yeats's paintings in the United States.

1955: In September Jack Yeats ceased to paint.

1956: *La La NOO* performed by the Lyric Players, Belfast.

1957: Jack B. Yeats died on March 28th.

A BIBLIOGRAPHY OF THE PUBLISHED WRITINGS OF JACK B. YEATS

by Martha Caldwell

BOOKS

Sligo. London: Wishart and Company, 1930.

Sailing Sailing Swiftly, London: Putnam, 1933.

The Amaranthers. London and Toronto: W. Heinemann, Ltd., 1936.

The Charmed Life. London: Routledge, 1938.

Ah Well, A Romance in Perpetuity. London: Routledge, 1942; see also *The Bell*, I, No. 4 (January, 1941) 37ff. and I, No. 5 (February, 1941) 62ff.

And To You Also. London: Routledge, 1944.

The Careless Flower. London: The Pilot Press, 1947; see also *The Bell*, I, No. 1 (October, 1940) 54ff. and *The New Alliance*, I, No. 4 (June-July, 1940) 5-6; I, No. 5 (August-September, 1940) 9-10; II, No. 1 (December, 1940-January, 1941) 7-8; II, No. 3 April-May, 1941) 6-7; II, No. 5 (August-September, 1941) 5-7; III, No. 3 (April-May, 1942) 6-7; III, No. 6 (October-November, 1942) 5-7; V, No. 1 (January-February, 1944) 5-7. *Dublin Magazine XV* (October-December, 1940), No. 4, New Seve, pp. 8-11; XVII, No. 1 (January-March, 1942) pp. 41-47.

PLAYS

Apparitions. (contains three plays: 'Apparitions', 'The Old Sea Road', and 'Rattle'). London: Jonathan Cape, 1933.

La La NOO. Dublin: The Cuala Press, 1943; also published in *The Genius of the Irish Theatre*. Edited by Sylvia Barnette, Morton Berman, and William Burto. New York: A Mentor Book (The New American Library of World Literature, Inc.), 1960, 212-244.

In Sand. Edited by Jack MacGowran, Dublin: The Dolmen Press, 1964; this book also contains 'The Green Wave', a one act conversation piece.

(Another play, 'Harlequin's Position', was performed in Dublin in 1939 but has not been published. 'La La NOO' was performed in 1942 and 'In Sand' in 1949, both in Dublin.)

BOOKS FOR CHILDREN AND FOR THE MINIATURE STAGE

James Flaunty or The Terror of the Western Sea. London: Elkin Mathews, 1901.

The Treasure of the Garden: A Play in the Old Manner. London: Elkin Mathews, 1902.

The Scourge of the Gulph. London: Elkin Mathews, 1903; also published in Paul McPharlin, *A Repertory of Marionette Plays.* New York: The Viking Press, 1929, 12-28.

The Bosun and the Bob-Tailed Comet. London: Elkin Mathews, 1904.

A Little Fleet. London: Elkin Mathews, 1909 (some poems by John Masefield are included in this book).

There are several unpublished plays for the miniature stage.

ARTICLES

'An Irish Race Meeting', *The Daily Graphic,* August 29, 1890, 14 (signed JBW, Rosses Point, Sligo, Ireland).

'A Cycle Drama', *The Success,* September 7, 1895, 108.

'The Great White Elk', *Boy's Own Paper,* Christmas issue, 1895, 36-37.

'Racing Donkeys', *The Manchester Guardian,* August 26, 1905 (this article is preceded by one entitled 'Whippet Racing' written by John Masefield and illustrated by Jack Yeats in the August 19, 1905 edition of *The Manchester Guardian*).

'Shove Halfpenny', *The Manchester Guardian,* October 4, 1905, 5.

'Drawings of Life in Manchester: The Melodrama Audience', *The Manchester Guardian,* December 9, 1905, 7.

A series of short articles accompanying illustrations appeared in *The Manchester Guardian* in 1906:

    'A Canal Fleet', March 31, 1906, 7

    'The Jumpers', April 7, 1907, 7

    'An Old Ale House', April 14, 1906, 5

    'The Concert House', April 21, 1906, 7

    'The Glove Contest', May 5, 1906, 7

    'The Cattle Market', May 19, 1906, 7

    'The Flat Iron', May 26, 1906, 7.

Synge and the Ireland of His Time by William Butler Yeats with a note concerning a walk through Connemara with him by Jack Butler Yeats. Dundrum: The Cuala Press, 1911; see also 'John

M. Synge', *The Evening Sun* (New York), July 20, 1909, *The British Nation* August 14, 1909, p. 7 and *J. M. Synge: Collected Works*, II, Edited by Alan Price, 'A Letter about J. M. Synge by Jack B. Yeats', London: Oxford University Press, 1966, 401-403.

'How Jack B. Yeats Produced His Plays for the Miniature Stage by the Master Himself', *The Mask, A Quarterly Journal of the Art of the Theatre* (edited by E. Gordon Craig, Arena Goldoni, Florence, Italy), V, No. 1, July 1912, 49-53.

'A Theatre for Every Man', *The Music Review*, (edited by R. Stuart Welch, The Riordan Press, 12 Noel St., Soho), I, No. 3, Autumn, 1912, 83-85.

'Modern Art', *Cumann Leigheacht an Phobail*, 1922, 1ff.; a similar article, 'Ireland and Painting', was published in *New Ireland*, IV, No. 11, February 18, 1922, 171-173 and IX, No. 12, February 25, 1922, 189-190.

'When I was in Manchester', *The Manchester Guardian*, January 2, 1932, 16.

'A Cold Winter and A Hot Summer in Ireland', *The Stork*, IV, No 14, March, 1933, London: Putnam, 27-29.

'Beach Made Models', *The London Mercury*, XXXIV September, No. 203, 1936, 425-427.

'Indigo Heights', *The New Statesman and The Nation*, XII December 5, 1936, 899-900.

'A Painter's Life', *The Listener*, XX September 1, 1937, 454-455.

'The Too Early Bathers', *The New Alliance*, I, No. 2, April, 1940, 3-4.

'A Fast Trotting Mare', *Commentary: The Magazine of the Picture Club*, I, No. 2, December, 1941, 5ff.

'Irish Authors: Jack B. Yeats', *Eason's Bulletin*, IV, No. 5, October, 1948, 3.

POEMS

'A 1,000 Miles to Rosses', *A Broadsheet*, April, 1902 (signed JBY).

'The Travelling Circus', *A Broadside*, No. 1, June, 1908 (No signature).

'The Adventurer's Oath from the Cardboard Drama of Esmeralda Grande', *A Broadside*, No. 11, April, 1911 (in manuscript among Yeats's papers).

There are a series of poems in *A Broadside* signed Wolfe T.

(Tone?) MacGowan (The spelling of the name varies). The name is written inside the cover of one of Yeats's sketchbooks done in 1913, and it is likely that it is a pseudonym for Jack Yeats.

'Bring Wine and oil and barley cake', *A Broadside*, No. 4, September, 1908.

'A Ballad on the Death of Mr. Israel Hands, executed for piracy', *A Broadside*, No. 4, September, 1908.

'Theodore to his Grandson', *A Broadside*, No. 8, January, 1909.

'O Irlanda, Irlanda', *A Broadside*, No. 4, September, 1911.

'Die We Must', *A Broadside*, No. 12, May, 1912.

'The Gara River', *A Broadside*, No. 3, August, 1913.

There is also a poem signed R. E. McGowan (Robert Emmet?): 'A Young Man's Fancy', *A Broadside*, No. 1, June, 1910.

There are two unpublished poems: 'The Lions at Lawrences' signed and dated Dublin, May, 1, 1942 (in manuscript form in Yeats's papers) and 'Hells Bells — are Ten in Number' (in manuscript form in the possession of Niall Montgomery, Dublin, Ireland). Among Yeats's papers there was a newspaper clipping on which he had pencilled his monogram; the clipping was of a poem, 'Dustbins' published in the *Irish Times*, May 8, 1931 and signed 'Constant Riser'. It may be that Yeats wrote this poem as well.

MISCELLANEOUS

Jack Yeats's publications include two sets of broadsheets: *A Broadsheet*, London: Elkin Mathews, 1902 and 1903; *A Broadside*, Churchtown, Dundrum: The Cuala Press, 1908-1915 (the initial copy was published by the Dun Emer Press, Dundrum).

A collection of drawings and paintings was entitled *Life in the West of Ireland*, Dublin and London: Maunsel and Company, Ltd., 1912.

Cartoons in *Punch*, both drawings and captions, were published by Jack Yeats using the pseudonym W. Bird, in 1896 and from 1910-1948.

A few lines were contributed by Jack Yeats in 'A Symposium on a Design by San Gallo for a Theatre', *The Mask*, XI, No. 4 (Oct., 1925) p. 160. And similarly a few lines of 'The Loveliest Thing I have Seen' *The Bell*, I, No. 2, Nov. 1940, pp. 40-43.

There are some unpublished epigrams (see *Printed Writings of George W. Russell AE: A Bibliography,* compiled by Alan Denson, London: Northwestern University Press, 1961, p. 207).

Jack Yeats wrote a review of a book by John Masefield — *Sea Life in Nelson's Time*, London: Methuen and Co., 1905; the review was published in *The Manchester Guardian*, September, 25, 1905.

Among Yeats's papers is the typescript of a talk 'For the Friends of the National Collection of Ireland' dated November 18, 1937.

THE TOWER SERIES OF ANGLO-IRISH STUDIES

III

JACK B. YEATS

A Centenary Gathering

edited and introduced by
Roger McHugh

This collection of homage to the art of Jack B. Yeats is issued to commemorate the centenary of his birth. These writings *by* Samuel Beckett, Martha Caldwell, Brian O'Doherty, Ernie O'Malley, Shotaro Oshima, Marilyn Gaddis Rose and Terence de Vere White are a tribute to the profound love of life which Jack B. Yeats expressed in his work. They include memories of the man, and assessments of his work. There are illustrations in line and a chronology and bibliography.

The Tower Series of Anglo-Irish Studies is published at the Dolmen Press in association with the Professor of Anglo-Irish literature and Drama, University College, Dublin. The Studies are concerned with the work of Irish writers whose contributions to world literature have been significant and the series, besides studies of a general nature, includes individual studies of writers and their work.

Roger McHugh is Professor of Anglo-Irish Literature and Drama at University College, Dublin.

A DOLMEN PRESS BOOK

published in association with
Anglo-Irish Studies, University College, Dublin

Distributed outside Ireland,
except in the United States of America and in Canada,
by Oxford University Press.

SBN 85105 205 3

£1.50 *net*